# On Common GROUND

## Worktext A

Project Manager and Editorial Director: Roseanne Mendoza
Editorial Associates: Jane Belenky Smith and Sally Conover
Photo Researcher: Gina Nonnenmacher
Cover art and design-related art: Jane O'Neal
Photographs from the *On Common Ground* series: Jane O'Neal
Artwork and maps: Max McDonald
Production/Electronic art: PC&F, Inc.
Acquired photos: See Photo Credits, pp. 163 and 164

Library of Congress Cataloging-in-Publication Data is available from INTELECOM.

Manufactured in the United States of America.

ISBN: 1-58370-050-1

03  02  01  00  5  4  3  2

# On Common GROUND
## Worktext A

**Writers**

**Sally Beaty**

**K. Lynn Savage**

**Beth Robinson**

**Kathleen Santopietro Weddel**

**Content Specialists**

**Roy Erickson**

**David Vigilante**

IN·TELE·COM
INTELLIGENT TELECOMMUNICATIONS

Pasadena, California 91105

# Table of Contents

## Worktext A

| | | Title | Theme | Story |
|---|---|---|---|---|
| 1 | 1 | Domino Effect | The reason for government; the purposes it serves | An angry citizen takes his problems to City Hall. |
| 15 | 2 | Like Taking Candy From a Baby | The U.S. Constitution as the basis for the rule of law | Police and city officials try to stop a scam whose victims are older immigrants. |
| 27 | 3 | For the Greater Good | Individual rights versus public or common good | Opinion is divided in the city when a construction project endangers homes in a Latino neighborhood. |
| 39 | 4 | Between a Rock and a Hard Place | Separation of powers among the three branches of government; the system of checks and balances | The city is in conflict with the federal government when the city doesn't have funds to follow federal guidelines for aiding disabled persons. |
| 51 | 5 | Collision Course, Part 1 | Freedom of expression and immigration | Because an anti-immigrant extremist plans to speak at a demonstration, the city must make difficult decisions about freedom of expression. |
| 65 | 6 | Collision Course, Part 2 | Freedom of speech; equal protection under the law | A father-son law team disagree about helping someone who gives hate speeches against immigrants. |
| 77 | 7 | A Delicate Balance | Freedom of the press | A reporter has information that could send a rapist to jail, but only if she reveals who gave her the information. |

| Turning Points | Find Out More | Inside Information |
|---|---|---|
| Events leading to the Revolutionary War | • What is government?<br>• Why is government important?<br>• What is the difference between limited and unlimited government? Between authority and power? | New World Waiting |
| Development of the U.S. Constitution | • What does "the rule of law" mean?<br>• What is the purpose of a constitution?<br>• What are the purposes of government?<br>• How is government in the United States organized? | Nation at War |
| Ratifying of the Constitution; creating the Bill of Rights | • What was the response to the new Constitution?<br>• How was the Federalist promise carried out?<br>• Bill of Rights | The Stars and Stripes |
| Principles that prevent the abuse of power | • What is federalism?<br>• How is power separated among the legislative, executive, and judicial branches of government? | Branches of Government |
| Reasons for immigration; patterns of immigration | • What does the Constitution say about freedom of expression?<br>• How has the desire for freedom of expression influenced immigration to the United States? | Symbols of a Country |
| A test case for the First Amendment | • Why did the Founders value freedom of speech?<br>• What are the benefits of freedom of speech?<br>• When is it difficult to maintain the commitment to free speech?<br>• Should free speech ever be limited? | Capitol Games |
| Freedom of the press— its importance and its limits | • What were some challenges to the press during colonial times?<br>• What is the role of the press today? | Executive Power |

# Acknowledgments

Developing a product of the magnitude and complexity of *On Common Ground* requires the dedicated, creative, and collaborative efforts of many people, working in tandem over a prolonged period of time. Only a few of their names can be singled out in the few lines that follow, but our gratitude to the team as a whole should be read into every word.

Special appreciation is extended to the

▶ leadership of INTELECOM, to members of the Board of Directors and Executive Committee, whose belief in the *On Common Ground* project gave it life

▶ United States Department of Justice, Immigration and Naturalization Service, and the Departments of Education of California, Florida, and New York for critical developmental and financial support

▶ National Leadership Council for Distance Learning and Adult Education and the U.S. Department of Education for taking the lead in developing the infrastructure to optimize distributed learning options for adults through the use of telecommunications technologies

▶ Center for Civic Education and Charles N. Quigley, Executive Director, for contributing the basic ideas of American constitutional democracy set forth in the Center's *We the People, The Citizen and the Constitution*

▶ National Center for History in the Schools, the Curriculum Task Force and the National Council for History Standards for guidance in developing the Turning Points segments and the worktexts

▶ video production team that did not back away from creating rich episodes that engage and challenge learners

The National Standards for Civics and Government and the National Standards for United States History provided the conceptual framework for *On Common Ground*. The major themes for the series—recommended by state leaders responsible for citizenship education, master teachers, and curriculum specialists—were reviewed by key government leaders, public officials, and immigration policy specialists including Dr. Lawrence Fuchs, Brandeis University, whose insights and suggestions were particularly valuable.

As the series moved into production, *On Common Ground* was shaped and molded, episode-by-episode and chapter-by-chapter, by the National Academic Council. This distinguished panel of educators—specialists in the fields of civics, history, and adult education—includes

▶ GLENDA ANDERSON—Adult Education Coordinator, ESOL and ABE, for 16 Technical, Adult and Community Education Centers, Orange County Public Schools Workforce Education Department, Florida

▶ ROY ERICKSON—Director of Justice Education Programs for the Center for Civic Education; California Coordinator for the Center's *We the People, the Citizen and the Constitution*; author; program director for major grant projects; past president of the National Social Studies Supervisors Association

▶ PATRICIA MOONEY GONZALEZ—ESOL Specialist, New York State Department of Education, Office of Workforce Preparation and Continuing Education; academic advisor and co-author of Worktexts and Photo Stories for *Crossroads Café*

▶ BETH ROBINSON—principal consultant, Adult Education and Even Start for her state; leader in developing programs that serve immigrants and refugees

▶ ADRIANA SANCHEZ-ALDANA—ESL/Citizenship Resource Teacher for Sweetwater Union High School District, California; developer of training package used throughout the state to educate teachers and tutors new to citizenship instruction

▶ K. LYNN SAVAGE—Instructor, City College of San Francisco; author and curriculum designer; lead academic advisor for *Crossroads Café*, teacher training specialist; 1998 recipient of Heinle & Heinle Publishers' Lifetime Achievement Award

▶ DAVID VIGILANTE—Associate Director, National Center for History in the Schools; member, Curriculum Task Force that developed History Standards; co-editor of *Bring History Alive!*; developer of curricular materials for National Center, Library of Congress, Huntington Library, and New York Times *Live from the Past* series

▶ KATHLEEN SANTOPIETRO WEDDEL—Adult Basic Education consultant for the Colorado Department of Education and others; author of skill-based textbooks and teacher training materials

Three members of the Council—Lynn Savage, Beth Robinson, and Kathy Santopietro Weddel—accepted the responsibility of developing the *On Common Ground* worktexts with Sally Beaty. Their creativity and commitment are reflected n the pages of this worktext. So, too, is the help and advice they received from other members of the NAC, as they linked the key concepts of each episode's dramatic story and documentary to the printed word—reinforcing the lesson's themes, fostering inquiry, and extending learning.

The transformation of the manuscript to finished product was guided by Roseanne Mendoza, who played a dual role as editorial director and production manager with extraordinary skill. She was ably assisted in this process by Jane Belenky Smith of INTELECOM and Sally Conover, ESL specialist. The production stills captured by Jane O'Neal, the imaginative sketches of Max McDonald, and the indefatigable photo research of Gina Nonnenmacher added immeasurably to the finished product.

Heartfelt appreciation to each of you, named and unnamed, who made *On Common Ground* a reality!

Sally Beaty, President
INTELECOM

These pages explain what the *On Common Ground* program is and how to use it. If you are not sure about how to use the program after you read this material, ask someone to discuss it. If you start with a clear idea of how to use *On Common Ground*, your chances for success will be excellent.

## What Is *On Common Ground*?

*On Common Ground* is a different and exciting way to learn about U.S. history and government. If you are new to the United States, it is also an excellent way to gain the knowledge necessary to pass the citizenship test. In this learning venture, the television episodes will show you democracy in action. The worktexts will help you understand the key concepts—the most important ideas behind those actions.

### The Television Episodes
Each of the 15 thirty-minute episodes includes an action-filled story and a short documentary segment. The stories take place in a typical American city. They show the "common ground"—the common values that people in the United States share. You will see the difference that individuals can make by exercising their rights as citizens. But each story is more than just an interesting drama. It is also an example of a concept that is central to American democracy.

The pictures below show the main characters in the stories.

### The Worktexts
There are two worktexts that provide learning activities related to the television episodes. Worktext A includes Episodes 1 through 7; Worktext B includes Episodes 8 through 15. The worktexts help you better understand what you hear and see in the videos. They also provide more information and activities so that you can be an active learner by thinking, talking, reading, and writing about what you hear and see.

## How Do I Use the Video Programs?

Watch each episode again and again. If you are watching the programs on television, you can record them and watch as many times as you like. The television programs and videos have closed captions, so that you can see the words the characters say on the screen. Watch without the captions first to get the general idea. Try to guess the meaning of words you don't understand. Then, if you need to see those words, watch again with the captions on.

## Questions

Here are some questions learners often ask about *On Common Ground*.

Carla Castillo
TV News Reporter

Marty Siegel
Assistant District
Attorney

Diane Clayton
Community Relations

Derek Powell
Assistant to the Mayor

Jess Holcomb
City Attorney

Jenny Tang
Receptionist

Mayor Reilly

### What Do the Liberty Bells Mean?

The Worktext activities are marked with one, two, or three liberty bells that indicate three levels of difficulty.

In each section of the worktext, do as many of the different level activities as you can. For example, in "Remember the Story," maybe you can do the level-one and the level-two activities easily. However, you may not be able to complete the level-three activity. So stop after the second level and move to the next section, "Remember Turning Points." Maybe here you can do all three levels easily, or you may be able to do only the level-one activity. But always begin with the level-one activity. And remember—if you have problems with an activity, get help from your teacher, tutor, study partner, or someone else.

### If I Need Help, Where Do I Go?

Work with a study partner—another learner, relative, friend, neighbor, or coworker. Your study partner can be someone who knows more English or more about U.S. history and government than you do. But anyone who is interested in talking about the ideas in *On Common Ground* can be a good study partner. Here are three things you can do with your partner:

▶ Talk about the video story.
▶ Ask questions about things you don't understand.
▶ Compare your activity answers and share your ideas and experiences.

## What Do I Need to Know About Using Each Section in the Worktexts?

The worktexts have activities for you to do before and after you watch each episode. Here are some suggestions for using the different sections in the worktexts.

### Before You Watch

These sections will introduce what happens in the story and the ideas presented in "Turning Points."

First, study the picture or pictures on the *opening page* of the unit. What do you think the story is about? Next, read the information below the picture.

Look at the six pictures on the "Preview the Story" page. These pictures provide an idea of what the story is about. Then read the questions and think about the answers you would give before you turn on your television set

Read the information and look at the pictures in "Preview Turning Points." Think about the questions

at the bottom of the page and share your answers with your study partner or someone else who is interested in the series.

### After You Watch

After "Remember the Story," you will do these activities.

🔔 Read what people said, then write who said it to whom. This helps you remember people in the story and why they are important.

🔔🔔 Read several paragraphs that tell the story and put them in order. Then match underlined words in the paragraphs with their definitions. These words will help you understand key concepts.

🔔🔔🔔 Work with a partner to role-play a conversation between two people from the story.

In the next section of the worktext, "Remember Turning Points," you will do these activities.

🔔 Check whether you understand information from Turning Points by marking sentences true or false, matching items, or categorizing items.

🔔🔔 Put words and phrases into a chart or timeline that shows how something you heard or read is organized.

🔔🔔🔔 Complete a chart using your own words and adding new information from your experience or your learning.

"Making Connections" will help you connect the story to "Turning Points."

### Getting Additional Information

"Find Out More" is a section with a reading and activities that expand on the theme of the unit. Work through this section following these steps:

▶ In "Find Out More: Reading," look at the illustrations and read the section headings. Think about the questions and ask yourself what the reading could be about.
▶ Read the selection. After you finish each section, try to answer the question in your own words.
▶ Notice how the words in darker type in the reading are used. Try to guess what each word means. Check your definitions against the glossary in the back of the book. For extra practice, you may want to make a new sentence with each word.
▶ Finally, answer the questions in "Find Out More: Key Ideas."

"Inside Information" focuses on topics such as holidays, qualifications to hold elected office, or U.S. coins with famous people on them. This is an activity to have fun with—often a crossword puzzle, a word search, or a short, interesting reading.

### Using the Information

In "Pick Your Project," you choose from three different activities and share your results.

In *Community Matters: Interact!*, you will get information by talking to someone from a government agency or by watching a process related to government, like a trial. These activities are good for people who learn best by listening and talking.

In *In the News: Get the Facts!*, you will get information from reading newspapers or magazines or from listening to the news on radio or television. These activities are good for people who like to work alone and who learn best by thinking or analyzing.

In *Creative Works: React!*, you will have a chance to add your creativity to the theme of the unit. These activities are good for people who learn well from artistic and visual projects.

## Check Your Own Learning

Several sections at the end of the worktext help you check your learning after completing each episode.

After each activity, always use the "Answers for Exercises" to check your answers. When you miss an answer, review the video or worktext.

When you finish a unit, turn to the "Score Sheet for Answers for Exercises" and record your points. If you are part of a class, your teacher may want to see your scores for the exercises to help you with the answers you missed.

After you watch an episode and complete the worktext exercises for it, do the "Check Your Progress" section for that episode. This check-up review has three parts for the different levels.

In *Check Your Memory*, you will answer questions about key government, history, and civics concepts in the episode.

In *Make it Real*, you will use what you learned in the episode to explain an event or situation. To do this, you need to understand the key concepts you hve been exploring.

And in *You Be the Judge*, you will solve a problem by selecting the better of two solutions and then writing one more. These are interesting situations to talk about with a partner after you check your answers in "Answers for Check Your Progress" and record your score.

When you finish "Check Your Progress," turn to the "Answers for Check Your Progress" section for that episode. For any key concept questions you missed in "Check Your Memory," study the information in the *Review* column of the answer key. If you have questions, talk about them with your teacher. Then record your scores on the "Score Sheet for Answers for Check Your Progress."

In the "Rate Yourself" section, read the unit objectives and check how much you learned. Be honest when you answer. Your answers will tell your teacher or study partner if you need more help.

At the end of your worktext, you also will find a copy of the U.S. Constitution and a glossary of important terms. As you read or review those sections, always check the meaning of words related to law and government in this glossary.

# 1 Domino Effect

In the United States, government provides a way for people to work together. It protects the rights of people and promotes the common good.

*In this episode, an angry citizen takes his problem to City Hall.*

*What is government's role when people threaten other citizens?*

# Preview the Story

**Look at the pictures. Think about these questions. Share your ideas with someone.**

🔔 What do you see?

🔔 🔔 What are these people thinking? What are they feeling?

🔔 🔔 🔔 What do you think will happen?

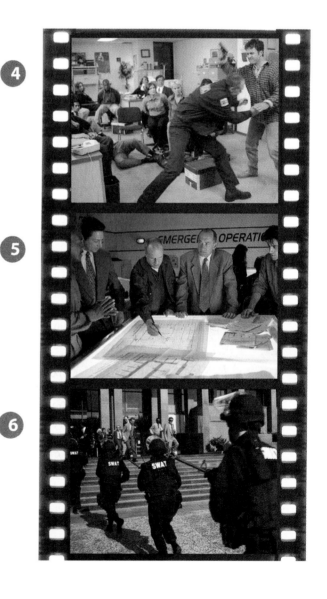

# Preview Turning Points

The need for government—for an organized way to protect individual rights and respond to situations that call for people to work together—is not new. In fact, the idea of government is almost as old as civilization itself.

**Think about the ideas above as you look at the pictures.**

**Think about these questions. Share your answers with someone.**

🔔 What kinds of services does government provide?

🔔🔔 What would life be like if there were no government at all?

🔔🔔🔔 Why is government important?

# Remember the Story

Read what people said. Look at the pictures. Complete the chart.

Eddie Buchanan
Hostage taker

Marsha Buchanan
Eddie's wife

Carla Castillo
TV news reporter

Tom Furlong
Negotiator

Vince Polito
Incident Commander

Mayor Reilly

Jenny Tang
Receptionist

TV audience

| What People Said | Who Said It | To Whom |
|---|---|---|
| 1. "Look lady. I'm a resident of the city. I am not leaving until I talk to the mayor." | *Eddie Buchanan* | *Jenny Tang* |
| 2. "If you came here to see me, why don't you let the rest of these people go, and we can talk?" | Mayor Reilly | Eddie Buchanan |
| 3. "I heard about the parking tickets and how you couldn't get to work this morning. I want to help you get out of this situation." | Tom Furlong | Eddie Buchanan |
| 4. "There is little known about the man holding the mayor and others hostage in City Hall." | Carla Castillo | T.v. Audience |
| 5. "Look, we had a chance to take him out, so we took it." | Vince Polito | Tom Furlong |
| 6. "Our son, David, died six months ago. It was a boating accident. Eddie's never forgiven himself or me, I guess." | Marsha Buchanan | Tom Furlong |

Put the paragraphs in order. Number them 1 to 6.

_5_ a. Tom Furlong is angry with Vince Polito. Buchanan thinks Furlong deceived him, and refuses to <u>negotiate</u>. The Incident Commander decides to attempt a rescue.

_1_ b. Eddie Buchanan is starting a new job after a long layoff. When he starts to leave for work, he finds a <u>citation</u> for unpaid parking fines and a parking boot on his truck. The truck cannot be moved. When he calls to say he will be late, his new boss tells him not to come in at all. Buchanan is very upset. He needs the job to pay his bills.

___6___ c. By going through the heating duct system, the SWAT team enters the mail room next to the mayor's office. They capture Eddie Buchanan, who is wounded in the process. As the ambulance takes the people who are wounded to the hospital, Mayor Reilly and his assistant leave <u>City Hall</u> to talk with reporters.

___4___ d. One <u>hostage</u> is not well. Diane Clayton and Mayor Reilly convince Buchanan to let <u>paramedics</u> rescue the sick hostage. As they leave with the sick man, one paramedic dives for Buchanan, who hits the paramedic in the head.

___3___ e. Buchanan uses the gun to hold people, including the mayor, as hostages. Police begin to <u>evacuate</u> the building. They call in Tom Furlong, a negotiator, to try to resolve the crisis. If Buchanan will not give up the fight, a Special Weapons and Tactics (SWAT) team, will try to rescue the hostages.

___2___ f. Buchanan goes to City Hall to get the boot removed from his truck. He asks if he can pay the fines gradually. When that doesn't work, he demands to see the mayor. He becomes angry when the receptionist says the mayor is busy. When the security guard comes, Buchanan fights with him and gets his gun.

**Write the underlined words in the paragraphs next to their definitions below.**

1. person kept by an enemy so that the other side will do what the enemy demands      _hostage._

2. order to appear in court      _Citation._

3. building where a city's government is located      _City hall_

4. to discuss something in order to reach agreement      _negotiate_

5. person trained to provide emergency medical help      _Paramedics._

6. to send or take all the people away from a place      _evacuate._

🔔 🔔 🔔 **Imagine that Carla Castillo interviews Jenny Tang after the SWAT team rescued the hostages. Role-play with someone. Your partner is Carla. You are Jenny.**

Ms. Tang, you were one of the hostages at City Hall today.

Yes, I saw Eddie Buchanan take the gun away from the guard.

CARLA CASTILLO:  Why did Eddie Buchanan take hostages?

JENNY TANG:

CARLA CASTILLO:  How did the SWAT team rescue you?

JENNY TANG:

CARLA CASTILLO:  What should the city do to make City Hall more secure?

JENNY TANG:

*Domino Effect*  **5**

# Remember Turning Points

Write **T (True)** or **F (False)** next to each statement.

_T_ 1. In the early 1770s, most people who lived in the thirteen colonies were citizens of Great Britain.

_T_ 2. The government of Great Britain wanted to tax colonists to help pay debts from Great Britain's seven-year war with France.

_F_ 3. The First Continental Congress decided to pay the increased tax to Great Britain.

_T_ 4. The delegates to the Second Continental Congress argued for independence from Great Britain.

_F_ 5. The Declaration of Independence does not apply to people in the United States today.

Number the facts in the box in order. Then write the darker words in the correct place on the time line. Check each event as you use it.

_6_ a. **Delegates** representing the colonies **sign** the **Declaration of Independence**.

_2_ b. The **British** government passes laws that **tax** the **colonists**.

_3_ c. **Colonial leaders** at the First Continental Congress **agree to stop trade with Great Britain**.

_1_ d. **Great Britain has a huge debt** from a seven-year war with France. ✓

_5_ e. **Delegates** at the Second Continental Congress **discuss independence**.

_4_ f. There is **fighting in Massachusetts** between the colonists and British soldiers.

### Events Leading to the Revolutionary War

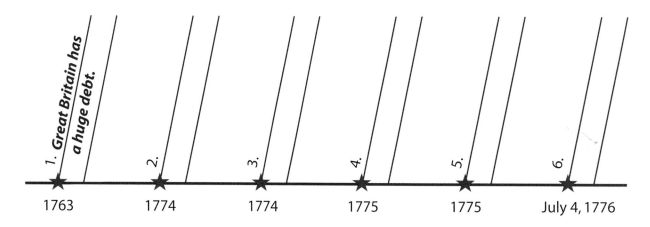

1. Great Britain has a huge debt.

| 1763 | 1774 | 1774 | 1775 | 1775 | July 4, 1776 |

**For each group in the first column, write the action the group took and the results of that action.**

| Group | Action | Result of Actions |
|---|---|---|
| 1. British government | *taxed colonists* | *colonists became angry about taxation without representation* |
| 2. First Continental Congress | | |
| 3. Second Continental Congress | | |

## Making Connections

**Read the quote below. Think about the questions. Share your answers with someone.**

> Government protects individual rights and responds to situations that call for people to work together.

1. In this story, who acts against the government?

2. Who in the government does he want to see about his rights?

1. How did the government protect the rights of these people?

    a. Buchanan

    b. the hostages

    c. Venderbook

    d. other citizens

Give examples from the story to support your answers.

1. What is the result of the government's actions?

2. How could the results have been different?

### What is government?

In a society, **government** consists of the people and institutions with authority to make, carry out, and enforce laws. Government also can settle conflicts about the law.

Mayors and city councils make, apply, and enforce rules and laws for their communities. Governors and state legislatures make, apply, and enforce rules and laws for their states. The president and congress make, apply, and enforce rules and laws for the nation. Courts at all levels of government apply and interpret laws, manage disputes, and punish lawbreakers.

### Why is government important?

Without government, life would be less organized. There would be no order to the way roads are built or towns and cities are planned. People might disagree about ways to settle arguments and deal with crime. There would be no coordinated methods for responding to natural disasters or defending the nation against attack. In other words, without government, people's lives, liberty, and property would be less secure. Government makes it possible for people to work together to accomplish things they could not do alone.

The basic purposes of government in the United States are to protect the rights of individuals and to promote the **common good**. Government establishes **law and order**, protects the **security** of the nation, provides agreed-upon public services, and maintains the basic ideals of **democracy**.

LAW AND ORDER

Government makes and enforces laws that protect our **individual rights** to ensure that people can have peaceful, orderly lives. Through the court system, the government also settles disputes and punishes lawbreakers.

NATIONAL SECURITY

The federal government provides for the common defense of the nation against outside attack. It also negotiates treaties with other countries. In these agreements, both sides agree to work together and support each other in case of attack.

## PUBLIC SERVICES

Government provides the services that cannot be accomplished without a **collective effort**—national, state, or local. Such efforts have resulted in a network of highways and roads, police and fire protection, and educational opportunities for all children.

## BASIC IDEALS

Government helps to maintain the basic institutions of society. It protects the personal, political, and economic rights of citizens. It guarantees rights such as freedom of religion and the right to a fair trial. It also provides many services, from basic health care to environmental safety standards.

**What is the difference between limited and unlimited government? Between authority and power?** *Not on test.*

Unlimited governments, such as authoritarian and totalitarian governments, are governments in which there are no effective means of controlling government power. In an **authoritarian government**, political power is concentrated in one person or a small group of people. Individual **citizens** and groups are **subordinate** to that power. **Totalitarian governments** go a step further. They attempt to control every aspect of the lives of individuals and forbid people to freely associate with one another to accomplish their goals.

**Power**, in relation to government, is simply the capacity to direct or control something or someone. The use of power can be good or bad, depending on how it is used. **Authority** is power combined with the right to use that power. This legitimate use of power usually comes from laws, customs, principles of morality, and/or the consent of the governed. When the police stop people who are driving too fast, they have both the power and the authority to do so. When a thief robs you at gunpoint, he has the power to do so, but not the authority.

🔔 **Use information in the reading on pages 8 and 9 to complete the sentences. Underline or highlight the sentence in the reading that supports your answer. Then write the sentence in the space below the choices.**

1. Government is people and organizations
   a. with the power to make and enforce laws.
   b. that support candidates for election.
   c. with the power to influence public opinion.

*In a society, government consists of the people and institutions with authority to make, carry out, and enforce laws.*

2. Government provides public services because
   a. people cannot perform them by themselves.
   b. they raise a lot of money for the government.
   c. people can easily perform them by themselves.

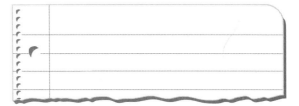

3. A totalitarian government does not
   a. allow people to meet freely.
   b. control how people behave.
   c. have powerful leaders.

4. Authority means
   a. the ability and wisdom to take action.
   b. the right and power to take action.
   c. the strength and power to take action.

🔔🔔 **Complete the sentences. Use your own words.**

1. In the United States, the responsibilities of the government are _____

   _____

2. Life without government would be different because _____

   _____

🔔🔔🔔 **Think about the questions. Share your answers with someone.**

1. Is government necessary in the United States? Why or why not?

2. What do you think are the characteristics of a good government?

# Pick Your Project

**Do one or more of the following activities. Share your work with someone.**

## Community Matters: Interact!

Visit the city hall in your local community. Ask questions like these.

▶ What offices are in city hall?
▶ How can I find offices within city hall?
▶ Who works at city hall?
▶ How can citizens arrange to speak to city officials?

## In the News: Get the Facts!

Collect at least three newspaper articles that show how government protects the rights of people and promotes the common good. Make a chart like the one below.

| Source and Date | Government Action | Benefits for People |
|---|---|---|
| **The Reporter December 14** | **Congress passes Resource Conservation Act** | **The law controls disposal of hazardous waste.** **Companies banned from disposal of waste in city dumps.** |

When you complete the chart, review ways that government protects people. Why is government necessary? How does government provide ways for people to work together?

## Creative Works: React!

Design a cover for the Declaration of Independence. Draw symbols or illustrations that represent the following ideas.

▶ All people are created equal.
▶ All people have rights to life, liberty, and the pursuit of happiness.
▶ All people have a voice in their government.

# Inside Information

## New World Waiting

The first people to see the New World of North America were the Native Americans. Some scientists believe they migrated from Asia to North America 2,000 to 30,000 years ago when the sea level was lower and a land bridge joined Siberia and Alaska.

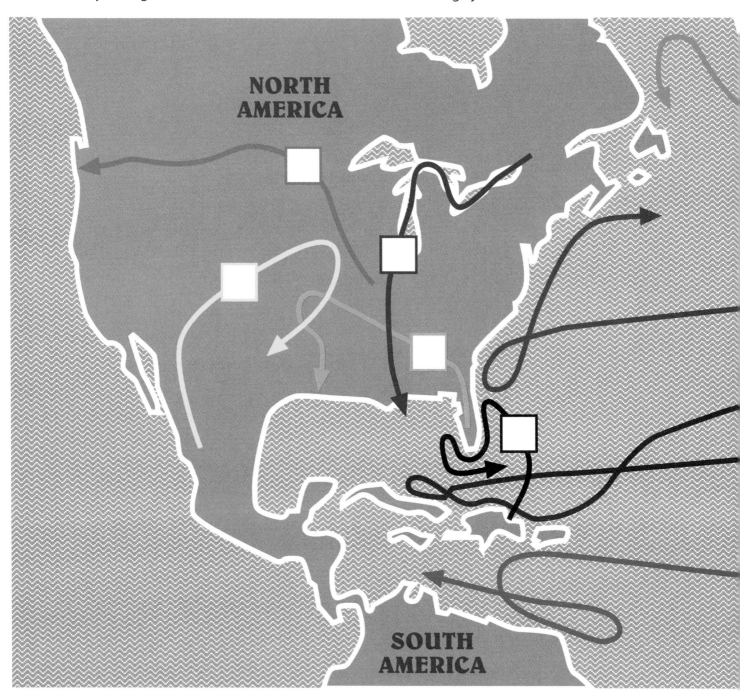

Time passed. Thousands of years later, from 900 to 1300 AD, the Vikings sailed from Scandinavia to western Europe, Greenland, and the coast of North America. Leif Eriksson founded the settlement of Vinland, what is now Newfoundland, but the settlement was abandoned after a few years.

The map below shows the routes of early explorers. Match the paragraphs on the next page with the routes the explorers took. Place the number of each paragraph in the appropriate box.

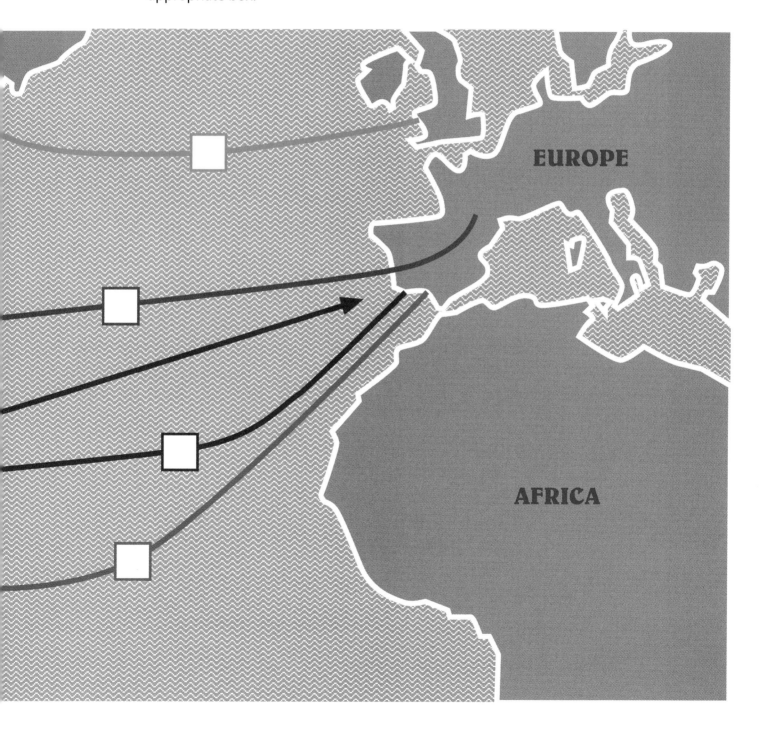

1. Christopher Columbus was looking for a shorter route to the East when he sailed from Spain in 1492 with eighty-eight men in three ships. In the early hours of Friday, October 12, 1492, after forty days at sea, one of his sailors saw land. Columbus thought he had reached India, but he hadn't.

2. In 1497, John Cabot, an Italian navigator sailing under the English flag, explored the northeastern shores of North America. His journey was important because it gave England a future claim in the New World.

3. The man who gave his name to the new continent was Amerigo Vespucci, an Italian navigator and chartmaker employed by Spain. He explored the American coast in the early 1500s, calling the land *Mundus Novus* or New World.

4. Spanish conquistadors came to find riches as well as land. Juan Ponce de León came searching for a fountain that could make old men who drank its water young again. In the spring of 1513, he discovered a land he called Florida.

5. In 1524, the King of France sponsored the expedition of the Italian sailor Giovanni da Verrazano. Verrazano sailed the New World coast from Florida to Newfoundland, and wrote about a certain harbor—a "delightful place, situated among steep hills." That place is now New York City.

6. The explorer Hernando de Soto set off from Florida to find seven cities of gold. Instead in 1542, with more than half of his men dead, he found a "great river," the Mississippi.

7. Later Francisco Vásquez de Coronado and his men marched from Mexico to Nebraska looking for the same seven cities without success.

8. In 1673, a Jesuit priest named Father Jacques Marquette and fur trader Louis Joliet traveled 2,500 water miles from the French area of Canada to the mouth of the Mississippi, claiming the center of the continent for France. Robert Sieur de La Salle followed in 1685, building forts and trading posts to strengthen the French claim.

9. After the U.S. purchased land from France in 1803, the government sponsored an expedition led by Captains Meriwether Lewis and William Clark to explore these new territories.

**Now check your progress on Unit 1, *Domino Effect*. Turn to page 130.**

# 2 Like Taking Candy from a Baby

In the United States, people live under the rule of law that is based on the Constitution.

*In this episode, some people try to cheat Jenny Tang's father. He needs help.*

*How can laws help Jenny's father?*

# Preview the Story

**Look at the pictures. Think about these questions. Share your ideas with someone.**

🔔 What do you see?

🔔 🔔 What are these people thinking? What are they feeling?

🔔 🔔 🔔 What do you think will happen?

# Preview Turning Points

People follow rules and laws every day. The Constitution is the basis for the rule of law in the United States.

**Think about the ideas above as you look at the pictures.**

1776

**Think about these questions. Share your answers with someone.**

🔔 What laws or rules relate to each of the pictures?

🔔 🔔 What laws do you have to obey in your daily life in the United States? What is the basis of these laws?

🔔 🔔 🔔 Why does a country need written laws?

# Remember the Story

Read what people said. Look at the pictures. Complete the chart.

Carla Castillo

Diane Clayton

Vince

Derek Powell
Assistant to the Mayor

Marty Siegel
Assistant District Attorney

Mark Taglioni
Assistant in D.A.'s office

Jenny Tang
Receptionist

Mr. Tang

| *What People Said* | *Who Said It* | *To Whom* |
|---|---|---|
| 1. "What these people are doing is illegal. There are laws that will protect you." | *Carla Castillo* | *Mr. Tang* |
| 2. "I've seen enough laws, enough government, in my life. I will solve this myself." | | |
| 3. "But what do you want me to do? The man signed a contract." | | |
| 4. "Maybe we can work our way inside their operation." | | |
| 5. "When the cash dries up, their house goes to me." | | |
| 6. "We have to get some help. Will you talk to someone?" | | |

Put the paragraphs in order. Number them 1 to 5.

_____ a. Mark Taglioni, Marty Siegel's new assistant, has another idea. He offers to work his way inside the <u>scam</u>. After convincing the loan company that he has experience swindling older people, Taglioni secretly videotapes the operation.

_____ b. But the tapes do not provide the evidence of <u>fraud</u> that the district attorney needs. Finally, Mr. Tang agrees to seek help. The next time someone from the loan company tries to collect money, detectives in a mobile van watch and listen. When Mr. Tang is threatened, the police enter the Tang home and make an arrest.

_____ c. Jenny's friends, Diane Clayton and Derek Powell, talk to Assistant District Attorney Marty Siegel about Mr. Tang's problem. Siegel says the city already has many cases that are better <u>documented</u>. Powell asks what happens if the <u>contract</u> Mr. Tang signed was signed <u>under duress</u>. That might help, Siegel says, but only if Mr. Tang asks for assistance.

_____ d. Jenny tells Carla about the scam. Carla tries to convince Mr. Tang that what the company is doing is <u>illegal</u>. But Mr. Tang doesn't want help, particularly government help.

___1___ e. Jenny Tang's father borrowed money from a lending company for his wife's medical bills. The company now holds a <u>mortgage</u> on his home, and keeps asking for more money. Jenny tries to help, but the pressure is affecting her job.

**Write the underlined words in the paragraphs next to their definitions below.**

1. agreement in which people borrow money to buy a house and pay it back gradually  _____

2. legal agreement between two or more people or companies that says what each side must do  _____

3. not allowed by the law  _____

4. illegal activity of deceiving people to gain money  _____

5. dishonest plan, usually to get money  _____*scam*_____

6. to do something because of illegal or unfair threats  _____

7. supported with evidence  _____

🔔 🔔 🔔 **Imagine that Jenny Tang talks to Assistant District Attorney Marty Siegel. Role-play with someone. Your partner is Jenny. You are Marty Siegel.**

Why did Mark Taglioni decide to work undercover?

Because we needed evidence that Vince was breaking the law.

JENNY: Why did you need so much evidence to arrest Vince?

MARTY SIEGEL:

JENNY: What will happen to Vince now?

MARTY SIEGEL:

JENNY: What can I do to protect my father from other scams?

MARTY SIEGEL:

# Remember Turning Points

**Write *T (True)* or *F (False)* next to each statement.**

___T___ 1. The U.S. Constitution, which was written more than two hundred years ago, is the basis for the rule of law in the United States.

___T___ 2. The Continental Congress established a weak central government in which each state had a single vote.

___F___ 3. The type of government created under the Articles of Confederation was a financial success.

___F___ 4. At the Constitutional Convention, large states wanted equal representation in Congress, but small states wanted representation based on population.

___T___ 5. The Constitution established a strong central government with a two-house legislature. *State of Representative House — Senate*

**Select a date—1776 or 1787—for each sentence. Then fill in the boxes to show whether the sentence applies to the Articles of Confederation or the Constitution. Check each event as you use it.**

**1787** a. **Authority is shared and controlled** by a system of checks and balances. ✔

*1776* b. **Congress has no authority to settle disputes** between states.

*1786* c. **Congress has no money or power.**

*1787* d. **Delegates compromise on** the basis for **representation in Congress.**

*1776* e. **States form a weak coalition** with no president or court system.

*1787* f. **Delegates agree on a strong** national **government.**

### Continental Congress and the Articles of Confederation (1776)

| _____ | _____ | _____ |
|---|---|---|
| | | |

### Constitutional Convention (1787)

| _____ | _____ | __a__ Authority is shared and controlled. |
|---|---|---|
| | | |

**Compare the government of the United States under the Articles of Confederation and under the Constitution. Read the list on the left. Write the change on the right.**

| Before the Constitutional Convention | After the Constitutional Convention |
|---|---|
| 1. a weak coalition of states | *a strong national government* |
| 2. a one-house legislature | |
| 3. no president | |
| 4. no court system | |

## Making Connections

**Read the quote below. Think about the questions. Share your answers with someone.**

> The rule of law is essential in a representative democracy.

In this story, who is accused of doing something illegal—of breaking the rule of law?

Who is responsible for enforcing the rule of law—the police, government officials, ordinary citizens, or all three of these groups? Give examples from the story to support your answer.

Does the rule of law protect victims, people who commit crimes, or both? Give examples from the story to support your answer.

**What does "the rule of law" mean?**

People in the United States are governed by a set of established, known, and accepted rules—laws that provide order and security. These laws govern people in positions of authority as well as ordinary citizens. No one is above **the law**.

Laws are used to do the following:

▶ describe how people should behave

▶ protect rights

▶ provide benefits

▶ assign responsibility

▶ limit the power of people in authority

The basis for the rule of law in the United States is the Constitution.

**What is the purpose of a constitution?**

Not all **constitutions** are alike. In some countries, constitutions simply describe the form of government. In countries ruled by a **dictator**, the constitution may have little real meaning. But in the United States, the Constitution does several things. It . . .

▶ describes the purposes and organization of government
▶ establishes government for the common good and protects the rights of people
▶ limits the power of government
▶ provides the framework, or structure, for the rule of law

## What are the purposes of government in the United States?

**Delegates** to a Constitutional Convention created the Constitution of the United States more than two hundred years ago. The **Preamble**, or introduction, states that the purpose of government in the United States is to do the following:

▶ form a more **perfect union**
▶ establish justice
▶ insure domestic tranquility (keep peace within the country)
▶ provide for the common defense
▶ promote the general welfare
▶ secure the blessings of liberty for ourselves and our children

## How is government in the United States organized?

*The founder fathers.*

The **Framers** of the Constitution wanted a strong national government with elected representatives. They established three branches of government—the **legislative branch**, the **executive branch**, and the **judicial branch**—each with different responsibilities.

*President*

**Executive power** was given to the position of president rather than to a committee of leaders. The powers and duties of the president are defined in the Constitution.

In establishing the judicial branch, the delegates created a **Supreme Court** and gave it the authority to interpret laws and to settle conflicts between states.

*Qust 21*

There were serious disagreements among the delegates about the legislative branch of government, the Congress. Finally, after much debate, the delegates accepted a compromise proposal. Congress would have a two-house legislature.

*house of Representative*
*Senate.*

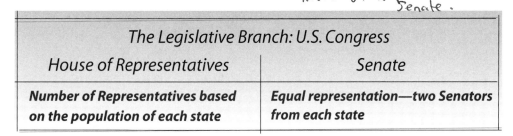

| The Legislative Branch: U.S. Congress | |
| --- | --- |
| *House of Representatives* | *Senate* |
| **Number of Representatives based on the population of each state** | **Equal representation—two Senators from each state** |

Four months after the Constitutional Convention began, the Constitution was completed. Thirty-nine delegates signed their names to its pages on September 17, 1787.

**Use information in the reading on pages 22 and 23 to complete the sentences. Underline or highlight the sentence in the reading that supports your answer. Then write the sentence in the space below the choices.**

1. In the United States, the rule of law applies to all people
   a. except justices on the Supreme Court.
   b. except the president.
   c. with no exceptions.

   *No one is above the law.*

2. The U.S. Constitution is
   a. the foundation for laws.
   b. a branch of government.
   c. a temporary document.

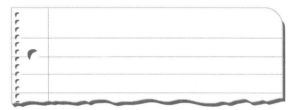

3. The Preamble to the Constitution states that one purpose of government is to
   a. establish one national religion.
   b. keep peace in the country.
   c. give all power to a few leaders.

4. The head of the executive branch of the government is
   a. a committee of leaders.
   b. the Supreme Court.
   c. the president.

**Complete the sentences. Use your own words.**

1. Three ways that laws are used in the United States are _____

   _____

   _____

2. The three branches of the U.S. government are _____

   _____

   _____

**Think about the questions. Share your answers with someone.**

1. How do laws control the way people behave?

2. What benefits and responsibilities do you have under the Constitution?

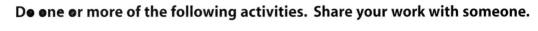

*Home work*

# Pick Your Project

**Do one or more of the following activities. Share your work with someone.**

## Community Matters: Interact!

Call the county clerk's office or the reference desk at the local library. Ask for the names and addresses of the two U.S. Senators from your state and the member of the House of Representatives elected from your district. Write the three names below.

| | | |
|---|---|---|
| U.S. Senator | U.S. Senator | Representative |

Find out some information about these people. What political party do they belong to? How many years have they been in office? When are their terms complete?

## In the News: Get the Facts!

Collect four stories from different news sources which demonstrate that the rule of law is essential in a representative democracy. Make a chart like the one below.

| Source | Action or event | What does it say about the rule of law? |
|---|---|---|
| **Channel 7 Nightly News** | **Supreme Court rules presidential line-item veto is unconstitutional.** | **The Constitution is the supreme law of the land.** |

Does each story give you a complete picture of what the rule of law means? If not, what is missing? What can you conclude about the importance of the rule of law in the United States?

## Creative Works: React!

Write a constitution for your neighborhood or the apartment complex where you live. Include the following information in your constitution.

▶ purpose of the constitution
▶ leadership of the neighborhood/apartment association
   a. roles for each office     b. selection process
▶ general rules and policies
   a. making sure they are followed     b. punishing people who break them
▶ how decisions are made
▶ how the constitution can be changed

# Inside Information

## Nation at War

The War for Independence between the colonies and Great Britain ended in victory for the colonies. They were now an independent country—the United States of America.

In the centuries that followed, the United States has been engaged in other wars. Although few of these conflicts have been fought on U.S. land, they have influenced the political history of the country. The chart below lists some of the major wars in which the United States has been involved. Fill in the missing information using your knowledge and experience, or library resources.

| Conflict | Years | Major Opponents | Results |
|---|---|---|---|
| The War of 1812 | 1812–1814 | United States vs. Great Britain | The United States remained independent. |
| The Mexican War | 1846–1848 | United States vs. Mexico | They took ha ff of the Mexican Land. |
| The U.S. Civil War | 1861–1865 | The North & South of the U.S. | Union of states preserved. Slavery ended. |
| The Spanish-American War | 1898 | United States vs. Spain | United States gained control of Puerto Rico, Guam, Philippines. |
| World War I | 1914–1918 | Allies (France, Britain, Russia, Japan, and later Italy [1915] and the United States [1917]) vs. Central Powers (Germany, Austria-Hungary, Turkey, Bulgaria) | |
| World War II | 1939–1945 | Germany, Italy, Japan called sttes axises vs U.S.A France England, U.S.A later Smaller countries. | Axis powers defeated. Territory and weapons taken from them. Money demanded for damages inflicted. Military leaders tried and punished. |
| The Korean Conflict | 1950–1953 | South Korea, supported by United Nations troops (including United States) vs. North Korea, supported by People's Republic of China | |
| The Vietnam Conflict | 1961–1975 | | Government of South Vietnam resigned. Country unified under North Vietnamese control. United States withdrew all troops. |

**Now check your progress on Unit 2, *Like Taking Candy from a Baby.* Turn to page 132.**

# 3 For the Greater Good

The first ten amendments to the U.S. Constitution protect individual rights.

*In this episode, Carla's father fights to save his community from a highway extension that the city needs.*

*What can people do when their individual rights conflict with the common good?*

# Preview the Story

**Look at the pictures. Think about these questions. Share your ideas with someone.**

🔔 What do you see?

🔔🔔 What are these people are thinking? What are they feeling?

🔔🔔🔔 What do you think will happen?

# Preview Turning Points

*assault in Battery*

> The United States added ten amendments to the new Constitution soon after George Washington became president. These amendments, called the Bill of Rights, protect individual rights.

**Think about the ideas above as you look at the pictures.**

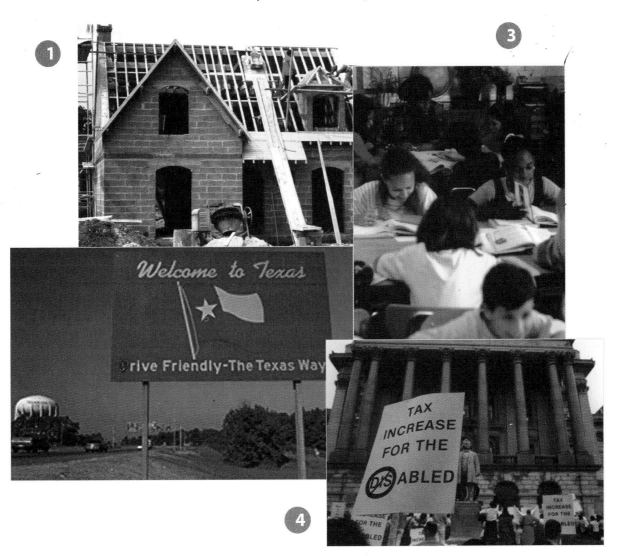

**Think about these questions. Share your answers with someone.**

🔔 Which pictures represent individual rights? Which do not?

🔔🔔 What rights are important to you? Have these rights ever been challenged? What happened?

🔔🔔🔔 Why are individual rights important in a democracy?

# Remember the Story

🔔 **Read what people said. Look at the pictures. Complete the chart.**

Carla Castillo

Juan Castillo

City Council

Ernesto
Moreno Heights Resident

Bill Garrison
Developer

David Malone
Developer

Mike Rodriguez
Councilman

| *What People Said* | *Who Said It* | *To Whom* |
|---|---|---|
| 1. "The Madison Highway project can help us become a real city for the first time, instead of separate neighborhoods." | **Bill Garrison** | **City Council** |
| 2. "Your highway will be like a knife that cuts the heart out of my neighborhood." | | |
| 3. "They are offering good money for my house." | | |
| 4. "If I support your plan, it will look like I've gone to war against my own district." | | |
| 5. "There are two men in the world I care about, and I feel like I'm stuck right in the middle." | | |

🔔 🔔 **Put the paragraphs in order. Number them 1 to 5.**

___1___ a. The <u>City Council</u> is considering a proposal for a highway extension that will cut through Moreno Heights. Bill Garrison, a businessman, speaks in favor of the project. Juan Castillo, Carla's father, speaks against it. After speaking to the council, Juan Castillo meets with his neighbors. Many have been offered money for their homes and businesses.

_____ b. Shortly before the vote, Carla learns that developers plan to finance Mike Rodriguez's <u>campaign</u> for mayor if he votes for the highway project. She tells her father. Juan Castillo tries to convince Rodriguez that there are things more important than political power.

_____ c. Developers try to convince Mike Rodriguez to support the highway project. Rodriguez is the councilman for the <u>district</u> that includes Moreno Heights. He says that the highway will destroy his old neighborhood. The developers argue that the project will be good for the city as a whole. They also remind him that he will need city-wide support if he runs against Mayor Reilly for the office of <u>mayor</u> in the next election.

_____ d. When the council votes on the <u>resolution</u>, the vote is tied. Then the last councilman, Mike Rodriguez, casts a "yes" vote. He later announces that he will run again for the city council, but not for the office of mayor.

_____ e. Carla Castillo interviews her father in his home for _Metro 5 News_. She asks him if there is some <u>compromise</u> that can satisfy both sides and move the project forward. As he begins to answer her question, Juan Castillo is hit by a brick thrown through the window.

**Write the underlined words in the paragraphs next to their definitions below.**

1. formal decision agreed on by a group after a vote    ~~compromise~~ · resolution·

2. official elected or appointed to be the chief executive of a city or town    major

3. group of elected officials responsible for making a city's laws    *city council*

4. series of actions intended to achieve a result, especially in business or politics    Campaign·

5. agreement that is reached after everyone involved accepts less than what they wanted at first    resolution · Compromise

6. section of the city divided for purposes of representation on the city council    district

🔔 🔔 🔔 **Imagine that Carla helps her father, Juan Castillo, move out of his house. Role-play with someone. Your partner is Juan Castillo. You are Carla.**

Carla, thanks for helping me pack.

You must be sad to leave this house.

JUAN CASTILLO: The new highway will destroy this neighborhood. Why didn't the City Council listen to us?

CARLA:

JUAN CASTILLO: I thought Mike Rodriguez would vote against the highway. Why did he change his mind?

CARLA:

JUAN CASTILLO: You try to be objective as a reporter. Now talk to me as my daughter. What is your opinion of the highway project?

CARLA:

# Remember Turning Points

Write *T (True)* or *F (False)* next to each statement.

___F___ 1. The Constitution created a strong federal government, unlimited in its power.

___F___ 2. When the Constitution was submitted to the thirteen states for approval, it received support from everyone.

___T___ 3. Opponents of the Constitution were concerned because it did not specify individual rights.

___T___ 4. As the debate continued, supporters agreed to add a bill of rights if the Constitution was approved.

___F___ 5. The Constitutional amendments, now called the Bill of Rights, were ratified three years later, the first of hundreds of amendments added to the Constitution.

Put the events in the box in the order in which they occurred. Then write the darker words for each event on the time line. Check each event as you use it.

___5___ a. **Congress approves** the **amendments** to the Constitution

___1___ b. The **Constitution** is **submitted to** the **states** for approval. ✓

___4___ c. James **Madison proposes amendments** to protect individual rights.

___2___ d. The **Constitution becomes** the **law** of the land after two-thirds of the states ratify it.

___7___ e. The **states ratify** the **amendments**.

___6___ f. The **last of** the thirteen **states ratifies the Constitution** and becomes part of the United States.

___3___ g. George **Washington is sworn in as** the first **president** of the United States.

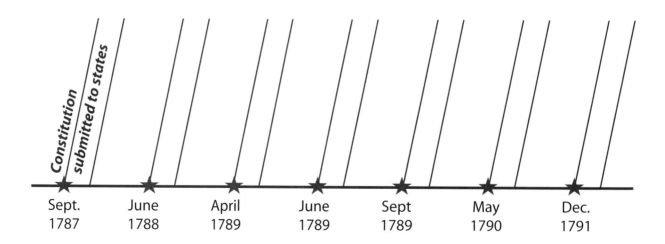

Constitution submitted to states

| Sept. 1787 | June 1788 | April 1789 | June 1789 | Sept 1789 | May 1790 | Dec. 1791 |

🔔 🔔 🔔 **Read the list of people and groups in the left column. Tell what each one did to help develop the Bill of Rights.**

| People and Groups | Role in Developing the Bill of Rights |
|---|---|
| 1. Opponents of the Constitution | *pushed for amendments that specified personal rights* |
| 2. Supporters of the Constitution | |
| 3. U.S. Representative James Madison | |
| 4. U.S. Congress | |
| 5. The states | |

## Making Connections

**Read the quote below. Think about the questions. Share your answers with someone.**

One of the primary purposes of the U.S. government is to protect the rights of each person. Opponents of the Constitution were afraid that a strong central government would threaten individual liberties.

🔔 1. In this story, what group thinks their individual rights are threatened?

2. Who represents these people on the city council?

3. Who leads these people in their fight to protect their rights?

🔔 🔔 1. What project is threatening the people's rights?

2. What rights are threatened?

3. How did these people feel about the project? What did each person do that showed those feelings?

    a. Juan Castillo        b. Mike Rodriguez        c. Carla Castillo

🔔 🔔 🔔 1. What happens in the end? Why?

2. What else might have happened?

## What was the response to the new Constitution?

When the Constitution was completed in September 1787, it was submitted to each state for a vote. The Constitution needed the approval of the people in nine of the thirteen states before it became the law of the land. Approval of the Constitution was also necessary before a state could become part of the United States.

The Constitution became the talk of each town and village. Newspapers wrote about it. People discussed it at public meeting houses and in churches. They argued about it on street corners and at home. And they elected delegates to vote on the Constitution at state conventions.

The supporters of the Constitution were called **Federalists**. They favored the idea of a strong national government to maintain order, regulate trade, and protect the rights of each state and its people. They were afraid that Spain, England, or France might overpower the young nation if it did not have a strong federal government.

The opponents of the Constitution, called **Anti-Federalists**, were afraid that a strong central government would threaten individual freedoms. They were troubled by the fact that there was no "bill of rights" in the Constitution. The Federalists felt this was unnecessary because the Constitution already limited government's powers. But they agreed to propose a bill of rights if the Constitution was **ratified**.

The debates in many state conventions lasted for months. The delegates suggested many **amendments**. Finally, in June 1788, New Hampshire became the ninth state to ratify the Constitution, and the new country was officially born. George Washington was elected president and inaugurated in 1789. In spring 1790, the last of the thirteen states, Rhode Island, approved the Constitution. What had been a loose union of independent states was now the *United* States of America.

## How was the Federalist promise carried out?

Shortly after George Washington became president, Representative James Madison from the state of Virginia reviewed the constitutional amendments proposed at the state conventions. Madison focused on proposals that protected individual rights. After months of debate, Congress agreed upon twelve amendments to submit to the states for approval. By 1791, nine states—the number required for ratification—approved ten of the amendments. They called these amendments the **Bill of Rights**.

# Bill of Rights

*The 10 first Amendement.*

**AMENDMENT 1:** *Freedom of Religion and Expression* Congress cannot establish an official religion or interfere with freedom of worship. It cannot prohibit free speech and other political freedoms.

**AMENDMENT 2:** *Right to Bear Arms* Citizens have the right to carry firearms for the defense of the country through a militia or national guard.

**AMENDMENT 3:** *Quartering of Soldiers* In times of peace, home owners do not have to provide housing for soldiers. During wartime home owners may have to provide housing for soliders, but only as prescribed by law.

**AMENDMENT 4:** *Security from Unreasonable Searches and Seizures* People and their property cannot be searched, or taken into custody, without a legal warrant.

**AMENDMENT 5:** *Rights of Due Process of Law* A person cannot be placed on trial for a major crime without a formal written charge. A person found innocent of the crime cannot be tried again for the same offense. A person accused of a crime cannot be forced to give evidence against himself or herself.

**AMENDMENT 6:** *Right to a Fair Trial* A person accused of a crime has the right to a speedy public trial before a jury of peers. The accused also has the right to a defense attorney and must be allowed to face and question witnesses.

**AMENDMENT 7:** *Trial by Jury* People have the right to a jury trial in civil suits involving more than $20.

**AMENDMENT 8:** *Fair Bail and Punishments* People cannot be charged unreasonably high bail fees or fines, or given cruel and unusual punishments.

**AMENDMENT 9:** *Rights Retained by the People* People have other rights in addition to those listed in the Constitution.

**AMENDMENT 10:** *Rights Reserved to States and People* The federal government has certain powers under the Constitution. All other powers, except those denied to the states, belong to the states or to the people.

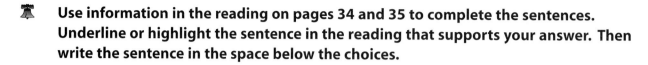

 **Use information in the reading on pages 34 and 35 to complete the sentences. Underline or highlight the sentence in the reading that supports your answer. Then write the sentence in the space below the choices.**

1. The Federalists
   - (a.) supported the new Constitution.
   - b. opposed the new Constitution.
   - c. feared a strong central government.

*The supporters of the Constitution were called Federalists.*

2. In 1790, the thirteenth state
   - a. approved the Bill of Rights.
   - b. ratified the new Constitution.
   - c. joined the Anti-Federalists.

3. The first ten amendments to the Constitution
   - a. are called the Bill of Rights.
   - b. were not ratified by the states.
   - c. are called the Madison Rights.

4. The First Amendment protects
   - a. the power of the central government.
   - b. states' rights to make their own laws.
   - c. people's right to choose their religion.

**Complete the sentences. Use your own words.**

1. It took a long time for the states to ratify the Constitution because _____

_____

2. The purpose of the Bill of Rights is to _____

_____

_____

**Think about the questions. Share your answers with someone.**

1. Why did the Anti-Federalists oppose the Constitution?

2. How does the Bill of Rights protect you in your daily life?

# Pick Your Project

**Do one or more of the following activities. Share your work with someone.**

## Community Matters: Interact!

Interview two people to find out their opinions about the Bill of Rights. You'll find the Bill of Rights, the first ten amendments to the Constitution, on pages 100 and 101.

Ask these questions. Take notes.

▶ Which rights are most important to you? Why?
▶ Which rights do you hear about the most? Where do you hear about them?
▶ Are there any unnecessary rights listed?

## In the News: Get the Facts!

Collect at least three newspaper articles about a situation in which individual rights conflict with the common good. Make a chart like the one below.

| Source and Date | Conflict | Opposing Positions |
|---|---|---|
| **Evening Press September 11** | **Control of the sale and possession of handguns** | MARK JONES, GUN CONTROL ADVOCATE: **"Violence in schools is increasing. Children under age ten are killing others. Handguns are in too many homes."** |
| | **Right to own firearms** | MARY BROWN, NATIONAL RIFLE ASSOCIATION (NRA) SPOKESPERSON: **"Every American has the right to own firearms. Personal property is not the business of government or society."** |

What does each side value? How do these values influence the position each takes? Why must decision-makers recognize conflict before proposing a solution?

## Creative Works: React!

After the City Council vote, Mayor Reilly proposes building a cultural center that will recognize and preserve contributions of people who have lived and worked in Moreno Heights for more than one hundred years. Use your imagination to create in words or pictures a display for the cultural center that honors the people of Moreno Heights.

# Inside Information

## The Stars and Stripes

No one knows who actually made the first official American flag. According to tradition, George Washington came to Betsy Ross's upholstery shop in Philadelphia in June 1776. He asked her to make a flag and showed her a rough pencil sketch he had drawn. She suggested a few changes, including the use of a five-pointed star rather than a six-pointed star. The flag that was created became the official symbol of the United States in 1777.

See if you can discover the answers to these questions about the U.S. flag.

1. Name the colors of the U.S. flag. _Red, White Blue_
   _Courage, truth, honor._

2. The designers of the flag wanted to honor the thirteen original colonies. How did they do this? _The stripes of the flag_

3. The designers also wanted to recognize each of the states in the United States in the flag. How did they do this? _With the Stars_

4. Which two states were the last two states to become part of the United States?
   _Hawaii 50th   Alaska 49th_

**Now check your progress on Unit 3, *For the Greater Good*. Turn to page 134.**

# 4 Between a Rock and a Hard Place

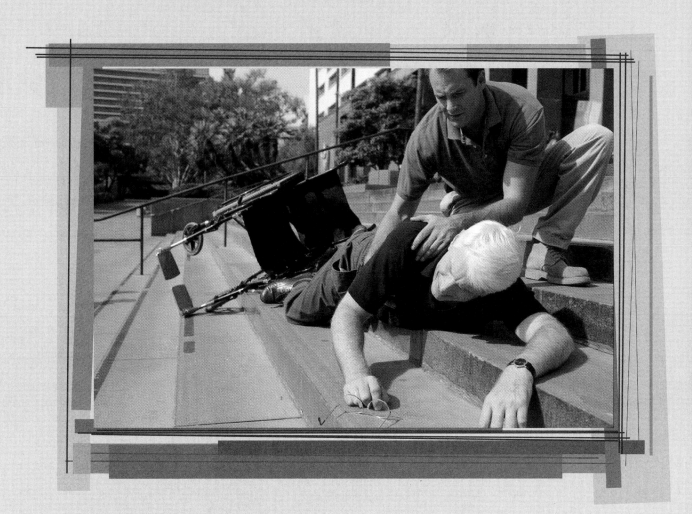

In the United States, the power of any one branch of government is limited. This division helps to prevent the abuse of power.

*In this episode, disabled people sue the city for not complying with a federal law that is expensive to implement.*

*How can the city resolve the problem without cutting other services?*

# Preview the Story

**Look at the pictures. Think about these questions. Share your ideas with someone.**

🔔 What do you see?

🔔 🔔 What are these people thinking? What are they feeling?

🔔 🔔 🔔 What do you think will happen?

# Preview Turning Points

The power of government in the United States depends on the consent of the people and on three principles that were established in the Constitution: federalism, separation of powers, and checks and balances.

**Think about the ideas above as you look at the pictures.**

**Think about these questions. Share your answers with someone.**

🔔 What types of governmental power and responsibility are shown?

🔔🔔 What examples have you seen of the separation of powers between federal and state governments? Among the three branches of government?

🔔🔔🔔 Why do you think it is important to have limits on the power of each branch of government?

*Between a Rock and a Hard Place* **41**

# Remember the Story

🔔 **Read what people said. Look at the pictures. Complete the chart.**

Councilman
Prescott

Derek Powell
Assistant to the Mayor

Jess Holcomb
City Attorney

James Wagner
Mitchell's son

Mitchell Wagner
Disabled Rights
Advocate

| What People Said | Who Said It | To Whom |
|---|---|---|
| 1. "We simply do not have the necessary funds to comply with it." | *Councilman Prescott* | *James Wagner* |
| 2. "You don't put enough value on the lives of disabled people to make them a priority." | | |
| 3. "All I'm suggesting is a delay, until the city can afford to follow the federal guidelines." | | |
| 4. "If we tell Washington no, this city is going to end up in court." | | |
| 5. "I'm not going to let them do this." | | |
| 6. "You're destroying everything I've worked for over the past twenty years. Why are you doing this?" | | |

🔔 🔔 **Put the paragraphs in order. Number them 1 to 5.**

_____ a. After the council meeting, Mayor Reilly talks with members of his staff. Derek Powell argues that the city cannot afford to follow the <u>federal guidelines</u> without sacrificing the safety of the community. City Attorney Holcomb disagrees. He doesn't want a legal conflict with the federal government.

_____ b. In response to the court <u>ruling</u>, Mayor Reilly tells reporters that the city will not <u>appeal</u>. He will review the city budget and consider other funding options to make the city more accessible to the disabled.

_____ c. Carla Castillo reports on the demonstration. People were arrested and charged with <u>obstruction of public property</u>. She announces the federal court's decision—that the city must comply with federal law regarding access for the handicapped.

_____ d. At the next City Council meeting, there is a <u>motion</u> to cut the police budget. This cut would provide the money necessary to make buildings accessible to handicapped people. The motion is defeated. The disabled coalition, led by Mitchell Wagner, plans a protest demonstration. The <u>coalition</u> also files a lawsuit against the city.

__1__ e. Mitchell Wagner falls from his wheelchair trying to go down the steps at City Hall. His son, James, talks at a City Council meeting about federal legislation that requires buildings to be safe and accessible for <u>disabled</u> people. A councilman says that the city will have to reduce the number of police to get money to <u>comply</u> with the legislation.

**Write the underlined words in the paragraphs next to their definitions below.**

1. suggestion made formally at a meeting and then decided on by voting

   _____

2. official decision about a legal problem

   _____

3. the act of preventing people from entering a public building or public land that anyone can use

   _____

4. specifications regarding how a law or regulation must be carried out

   _____ *federal guidelines* _____

5. ask a higher court to change a lower court's decision

   _____

6. follow a rule or law

   _____

7. unable to use a part of the body completely; handicapped

   _____

8. alliance of groups or people for a common goal

   _____

🔔 🔔 🔔 **Imagine that Derek Powell talks to Mayor Reilly after the demonstration. Role-play with someone. Your partner is Derek Powell. You are Mayor Reilly.**

James Wagner is not like his father.

His father believes in the legal process. James broke the law to make his point.

DEREK POWELL: When the fire alarm went off, I thought we had a disaster on our hands.

MAYOR REILLY:

DEREK POWELL: How can we comply with the federal court ruling?

MAYOR REILLY:

DEREK POWELL: If we cut police protection, people will protest.

MAYOR REILLY:

# Remember Turning Points

🔔 Match the branch of government with the responsibility. Write the letter on the line.

a. legislative        b. executive        c. judicial

___a___ 1. make laws

___c___ 2. resolve conflicts in court    *pages 6*

___a___ 3. develop policies

___a b___ 4. approve president's appointment of judges

___b___ 5. sign bills into law

___c___ 6. decide if president's actions are constitutional

🔔🔔 Read the words in the box. Write each word next to its definition.

| Checks and balances | Separation of powers | Federalism |
| --- | --- | --- |

| *Principles that Limit Government Power* | |
| --- | --- |
| 1. | division of power between the national and state governments |
| 2. | division of power between three different branches of government |
| 3. | the way each branch can limit the power of the other two branches |

🔔 🔔 🔔 **Complete the chart with functions for each branch of government and examples of how the power of that branch is limited.**

| Branch/Name | Function | Example of How Power is Limited |
|---|---|---|
| 1. Legislative **Congress** | • *makes laws* <br> • | • *The president can approve or veto the laws* |
| 2. Executive | • <br> • | • |
| 3. Judicial | • <br> • | • |

## Making Connections

**Read the quote below. Think about the questions. Share your answers with someone.**

> Under the U.S. Constitution, power is not only divided between federal and state governments. It is also divided among the executive, legislative, and judicial branches of government.

🔔 1. In this story, what law causes conflict among groups in the city?

2. Who made the law?

3. Why isn't the city enforcing it?

🔔 🔔 1. What is the difference in the ways James Wagner and his father try to get the city to enforce the law?

2. Why do they disagree?

🔔 🔔 🔔 1. How does the judicial branch resolve the conflict?

2. What else could each branch of the government do to resolve it?

Governmental power in the United States depends on the consent of the people and is shaped by three key principles established in the Constitution—the principles of **federalism**, **separation of powers**, and **checks and balances**.

## What is federalism?

The Framers of the Constitution created a federal system of government that gave only certain powers to the national government. Other powers were given to state governments and to the people themselves.

Federalism is a system that divides power between the states and the national government. It gives the federal government the authority it needs and, at the same time, it helps protect each state's rights. The federal government deals with issues that affect all citizens. Each state government serves the particular needs of people who live in it. The chart below shows how federal and state powers are different.

| *Federal Government* | *State Government* |
| --- | --- |
| Controls trade between states and with other nations | Establishes public schools |
| Declares and conducts war | Enacts regulations for driving on state highways |
| Prints and issues money | Passes laws related to marriage and divorce |

Certain powers are shared by federal and state governments. For example, both levels of government have the power to tax the people. Both have responsibility for the health and welfare of the people. But if there is a dispute, the Constitution and laws of the United States are the "supreme law of the land." This means that state governments and local city and town governments cannot make laws that conflict with the Constitution or with laws passed by Congress.

## How is power separated among the legislative, executive, and judicial branches of government?

The Framers of the Constitution believed that separation of powers and checks and balances were essential to protect the rights of the people. They gave different powers to the three branches of the national government. And they gave each branch ways to control the powers of the other branches.

| Branch of Government | Powers | Checks and Balances |
|---|---|---|
| **LEGISLATIVE BRANCH** Senate and House of Representatives | Makes laws. Bills passed by both houses of Congress become law with president's signature<br><br>Approves or rejects presidential nominations<br><br>Has responsibility for declaring war | If the president disagrees with some part of a bill, he or she can **veto** the bill. If two-thirds of both houses of Congress again vote in favor of the bill, it becomes law without the president's signature.<br><br>If the law unfairly limits basic rights of the people, the Supreme Court can declare it **unconstitutional**.<br><br>There is a limited term of office. Every two or six years, voters elect people to represent them as members of Congress. |
| **EXECUTIVE BRANCH** President | Enforces laws made by Congress<br><br>Nominates people for important executive and judicial jobs<br><br>Makes treaties with foreign nations<br><br>Serves as **commander-in-chief** in times of war | The actions of the president are subject to **judicial review**.<br><br>The Senate has the power to accept or reject these **nominations**.<br><br>The Senate must approve a **treaty** by a two-thirds vote before it goes into effect.<br><br>Only Congress can declare war and authorize the money to support it.<br><br>There is a limited term of office. Every four years, voters elect a president. No president can serve more than two terms.<br><br>A president suspected of committing a crime can be **impeached** by the House of Representatives and tried by the Senate. A president found guilty by the Senate is removed from office. |
| **JUDICIAL BRANCH** Supreme Court | Interprets the law<br><br>Settles conflicts between states<br><br>Determines whether laws or actions are constitutional | Judges are appointed by the president and approved by the Senate. Judges serve until they retire or die, or are removed from office by the impeachment process described above. |

Use information in the reading on pages 46 and 47 to complete the sentences. Underline or highlight the sentence in the reading that supports your answer. Then write the sentence in the space below the choices.

1. Under federalism, state and national governments have
   a. different powers.
   b. the same powers.
   c. unchecked powers.

*Federalism is a system that divides power between the states and the national government.*

2. Both state and national governments have the power to
   a. declare war.
   b. sign treaties.
   c. tax the people.

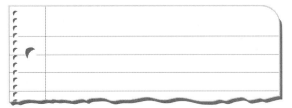

3. The legislative branch writes bills that become laws after
   a. the Supreme Court agrees.
   b. the president signs them.
   c. both houses of Congress act.

4. One check on the president's power is
   a. Congress can nominate judges.
   b. the Supreme Court can impeach the president.
   c. the Senate has the power to accept or reject the president's nominations.

Complete the sentences. Use your own words.

1. One power reserved for the federal government is _____

   _____

2. The power of Congress is limited because _____

   _____

Think about the questions. Share your answers with someone.

1. How do the three branches of government work together to create laws?

2. What are the advantages and disadvantages of a system with many checks and balances?

# Pick Your Project

*Hw.*

*Home work*

**Do one or more of the following activities. Share your work with someone.**

## Community Matters: Interact!

Contact the mayor's office of the city and ask for a schedule of city council meetings. Ask how you can get a copy of the agenda for the meeting you want to attend. Attend a meeting and watch the local legislative and executive branches in action. Think about these questions as you watch. Take notes.

▶ What is the role of the mayor?
▶ What is the role of the city council members?
▶ Can citizens speak at the meetings? How?

## In the News: Get the Facts!

Find three newspaper articles that illustrate the system of checks and balances among the three branches of government in the United States. Make a chart like the one below.

| Source and Date | Example | Checks and Balances |
|---|---|---|
| **Morning News November 8** | *President rejects bill to cut Medicare benefits. Congress may not have votes to override veto.* | *A bill passed by Congress does not become law without the president's signature.* <br><br> *Two-thirds of the Congress must vote for the bill again for it to become law without the president's signature.* |

In each case, which branch of government is doing the "checking" and which branch is being "checked"? Do your examples show a balance of power among the three branches of government? Why or why not?

## Creative Works: React!

Write a short play or prepare an audiotape of a skit with characters representing the three branches of government. You will want to have at least four characters: a president, senator, representative, and Supreme Court judge. Each character acts out his or her role showing how the branches interact.

# Inside Information

## Branches of Government

Use these words to describe the legislative and executive branches of government at national, state, and local levels.

| City Council | Governor | President |
| --- | --- | --- |
| Congress | Mayor | State Legislature |

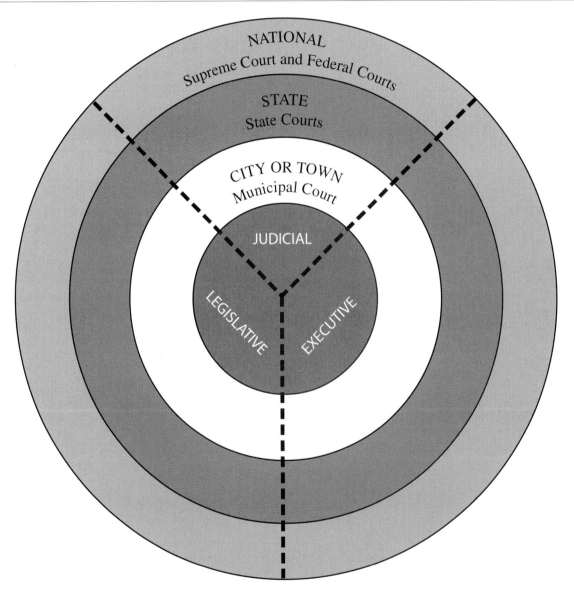

**Now check your progress on Unit 4,** *Between a Rock and a Hard Place.* **Turn to page 136.**

# 5 Collision Course, Part 1

Freedom of expression is an important right in a democratic society.

*In this episode, a political rally goes out of control.*

*How can a community protect people in these situations without violating freedom of expression?*

# Preview the Story

**Look at the pictures from each story. Think about these questions. Share your ideas with someone.**

🔔 What do you see?

🔔 🔔 What are these people thinking? What are they feeling?

🔔 🔔 🔔 What do you think will happen?

## The Matthews Family's Story

## Clay Sanford's Story

# Preview Turning Points

Many immigrants came to the United States seeking freedom of expression—the right to express ideas and beliefs without government interference.

**Think about the ideas above as you look at the pictures.**

**Think about these questions. Share your answers with someone.**

🔔 How do people express their ideas and beliefs?

🔔🔔 What are some cases you've heard or read about in which governments interfered with the expression of personal ideas and beliefs?

🔔🔔🔔 Why is freedom of expression important?

# Remember the Story

## The Matthews Family's Story

🔔 **Read what people said. Look at the pictures. Complete the chart.**

Diane Clayton

Linda Matthews
City employee

Paul Tremaine
Plant Manager

Ray Matthews
Unemployed
worker

Workers at plant

Jenny Tang

| What People Said | Who Said It | To Whom |
|---|---|---|
| 1. "The only way this company can remain competitive is by cutting our costs." | *Paul Tremaine* | *workers* |
| 2. "It's been two months. We can't go on like this." | | |
| 3. "My husband thinks Sanford has it all figured out." | | |
| 4. "I don't know what more I can do. I never thought things were going to turn out like this." | | |
| 5. "This isn't the time to give up. We've still got a life together." | | |

🔔 🔔 **Put the paragraphs in order. Number them 1 to 5.**

_____ a. The situation at home is beginning to affect Linda at work. She is upset when she hears Jenny tell Diane that people who listen to Clay Sanford are morons.

___1___ b. The manager of a large industrial plant tells a group of workers that to stay <u>competitive</u> the company must <u>contract</u> out some of its manufacturing to labor outside the country. The workers, including Ray Matthews, no longer have a job.

_____ c. Eventually, Ray's search for work takes him to a job counselor, who suggests a part-time job delivering pizza. Ray thinks that <u>welfare</u> would provide more support for his family than that job.

_____ d. Ray and his friends can't understand the company's decision. The company's last report showed a huge <u>profit</u>. Ray and his friends believe the real reason for contracting outside the country is to find cheap labor.

_____ e. Ray has been out of work and looking for a job for more than two months when he watches a news report about Clay Sanford and his anti-immigrant campaign. Ray's wife, Linda, doesn't want their son to hear Sanford's hate talk. Ray doesn't find anything wrong with Sanford's ideas. Linda suggests that Ray look for a job through a <u>temp agency,</u> but Ray says he needs <u>benefits</u> and more than <u>minimum wage</u>.

**Write the underlined words in the paragraphs next to their definitions below.**

1. determined to be more successful than other people or companies

   _____

2. to make an agreement to hire someone to do work    _____ *contract* _____

3. things such as medical, dental, and life insurance, provided by an employer

   _____

4. lowest rate that federal and state law allows an employer to pay an employee

   _____

5. business that provides the services of qualified workers to other businesses upon request, for limited periods of time

   _____

6. money left after deducting business expenses

   _____

7. money provided by the government to people who are temporarily in financial need

   _____

🔔 🔔 🔔 **Imagine that Linda Matthews talks to her husband Ray Matthews. Role-play with someone. Your partner is Linda Matthews. You are Ray Matthews.**

LINDA MATTHEWS: What do you mean?

RAY MATTHEWS:


LINDA MATTHEWS: He blames immigrants and bureaucrats for all our problems. How can you agree with him?

RAY MATTHEWS:


LINDA MATTHEWS: Will our lives ever be the same again?

RAY MATTHEWS:

# Remember the Story

## Clay Sanford's Story

🔔 **Read what people said. Look at the pictures. Complete the chart.**

Carla Castillo

Francisco Lopez
Attorney

Hector Lopez
Attorney

Crowd

Clay Sanford
Anti-immigrant
organizer

Dave Kinnard
Police Chief

TV audience

| What People Said | Who Said It | To Whom |
|---|---|---|
| 1. "We've allowed these immigrants to infect our national way of life and destroy everything that made this country great." | *Clay Sanford* | *Crowd* |
| 2. "Although numerous people were treated for cuts and bruises, there were no serious injuries, and police made no arrests." | | |
| 3. "We had no intention of denying Mr. Sanford the opportunity to say what he wanted. We were there for one reason: to ensure that the rally was peaceful." | | |
| 4. "I want to file a lawsuit against the city for violating my First Amendment rights, and I'd like this law firm to represent me." | | |
| 5. "My father and I have worked too hard to be a part of something like this." | | |

🔔 🔔 **Put the paragraphs in order. Number them 1 to 5.**

_____ a. At the rally, Sanford says immigrants have destroyed everything that made the country great. Many people applaud, but some boo. People begin to push and shove. Sanford has a <u>permit</u>, but police stop the rally because of the disturbance.

_____ b. Francisco Lopez doesn't want to represent Sanford. He doesn't like his views about immigrants. But if he says no, it will look like his firm <u>discriminates</u> against Sanford.

_____ c. Mayor Reilly wants to cancel the rally to avoid a <u>riot</u>. The city attorney says, "You can't <u>suspend</u> the guy's First Amendment rights because something *might* happen."

__1__  d. Clay Sanford travels around the country making speeches against immigration. He says that "foreigners" take jobs away from "real" Americans. The mayor is worried. The city has a lot of unemployed workers and a large immigrant population. He doesn't want the immigrants to become <u>scapegoats</u>.

_____  e. Because police stopped the rally, Sanford believes his right of <u>free speech</u> was denied. He asks the father-and-son law firm of Francisco and Hector Lopez to represent him in a lawsuit against the city. Francisco is a leading authority on constitutional law.

**Write the underlined words in the paragraphs next to their definitions below.**

1. official written document giving someone the right to do something                   *permit*

2. uncontrolled violent behavior by a large group      _____

3. right to verbally express beliefs without government interference      _____

4. stop or take away, usually temporarily      _____

5. treats unfairly because of prejudice based on race, sex, religion, age, or nationality      _____

6. people blamed for something that is done by others or by a whole group      _____

🔔 🔔 🔔   **Imagine that Clay Sanford's assistant talks to him before their next rally. Role-play with someone. Your partner is Clay Sanford's assistant. You are Sanford.**

ASSISTANT:  Is the plan the same? Do we stage another protest?

CLAY SANFORD:

ASSISTANT:  How did you convince Francisco and Hector Lopez to represent you?

CLAY SANFORD:

ASSISTANT:  Now the city knows about our lawsuit. How will the police react at the rally next week?

CLAY SANFORD:

# Remember Turning Points

🔔 **Match each group with a statement. Write a letter on the line. Some statements may have more than one answer. Some letters may be used more than once.**

a. Africans      b. Asians      c. Europeans

d. Spaniards and Mexicans      e. Native Americans      f. Latin Americans

**e** 1. These people were the earliest inhabitants of the land that is now the United States.

**c** 2. These early immigrants were seeking religious and political freedom and economic opportunities.

**a** 3. In the 1600s and 1700s, most of these immigrants were brought to the United States as slaves.

**b** 4. The first of these immigrants had heard about the discovery of gold in California and wanted to earn money for their families.

**d** 5. When the United States added new territory in the 1800s, these people became U.S. citizens.

**b** 6. The immigration of these people to the United States was restricted from the late 1800s to the mid-1900s.

**f a b d** 7. In recent decades, large numbers of these people have immigrated to the United States.

🔔🔔 **Below is a timeline that shows different groups of immigrants and some of their reasons for coming to the United States. Write each group from the box in the appropriate place on the timeline. Check each one after you use it.**

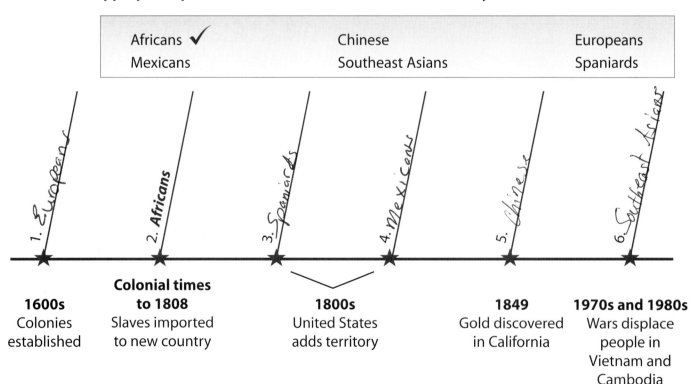

| Africans ✓ | Chinese | Europeans |
| Mexicans | Southeast Asians | Spaniards |

1. Europeans
2. Africans
3. Spaniards
4. Mexicans
5. Chinese
6. Southeast Asians

**1600s**
Colonies established

**Colonial times to 1808**
Slaves imported to new country

**1800s**
United States adds territory

**1849**
Gold discovered in California

**1970s and 1980s**
Wars displace people in Vietnam and Cambodia

🔔 🔔 🔔 **In the left column, read the reasons people immigrated to the United States. Then in the right column, write the names of all the groups that immigrated for each reason.**

| Reasons for Immigrating | Groups |
|---|---|
| 1. fleeing persecution and seeking religious freedom | **Europeans in the 1600s** |
| 2. escaping revolution and political persecution | |
| 3. seeking economic opportunities and better living conditions | Cuban, North Koreans Asians. |

## Making Connections

**Read the quote below. Think about the questions. Share your answers with someone.**

> A poet once called the United States a nation of nations—
> a country populated by people of many different races, religions,
> languages, and ethnic backgrounds.

🔔 1. In this story, whose message opposes immigration?

2. To whom does the message appeal?

3. What groups of people are divided by this message?

🔔 🔔 1. What message is expressed?

2. What happens at the rally?

🔔 🔔 🔔 1. What does Sanford decide to do after the rally? Why?   Sue the city
1st amendement rights were denied
2. Who does he get to represent him?
   Mr. Lopez
3. What else could have happened?

### What does the Constitution say about freedom of expression?

The Preamble to the Constitution establishes a basic purpose for government in the United States. That purpose is to "secure the blessings of liberty to ourselves and our **posterity**." The Framers of the Constitution weren't looking only for freedom for themselves. They wanted freedom also for future generations.

Many personal freedoms guaranteed by the Constitution are found in the words of the First Amendment:

*Congress shall make no law abridging the freedom of speech, or of the press; or the right of the people peaceably to assemble, and to petition the government for a redress of grievances.*

In simple language, this means that Congress cannot pass a law that limits these rights or freedoms:

- ▶ freedom of speech
- ▶ freedom of the press
- ▶ freedom to gather peacefully
- ▶ freedom to ask government to correct wrongs

Together these four rights make up **freedom of expression**. They are four different ways to express ideas and beliefs.

### How has the desire for freedom of expression influenced immigration to the United States?

From its beginnings, the United States has been what the great nineteenth-century poet Walt Whitman called "a nation of nations." It is a country of millions of **immigrants** representing different races, religions, languages, and ethnic backgrounds.

Reasons for immigrating to the United States are as varied as the people themselves. Many people are trying to escape **persecution**. They are looking for freedoms they were denied in their homelands.

Many early immigrants to the land that later became the United States were Europeans. The Spanish established a fort at St. Augustine, Florida, in 1565. They had explored as far north as South Carolina before British settlers arrived at Jamestown and Plymouth.

In the 1600s, England's plan for establishing an overseas colony attracted many settlers to the New World. Advertisements were full of promises. But all the settlers wanted was the chance to own their own land.

Shiploads of immigrants arrived. The Massachusetts Bay Colony became home to Puritans trying to escape persecution by the Church of England. The colony of Maryland became a **refuge** for Roman Catholics. New Jersey offered land grants, freedom of religion, and representative government to immigrants.

In the 1700s, new groups of immigrants arrived from Germany and Ireland. Many of these settlers had left their countries because of religious and economic problems, too. The degree of religious **tolerance** they found in the new country was unusual for its time. Unlike many countries of Europe, no single religion dominated the colonies as a whole.

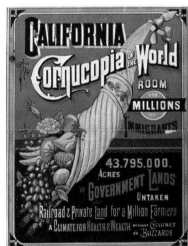

The 1800s brought immigrants from Central and Eastern Europe, many escaping political and economic oppression. Irish, Italian, and Greek farmers suffering from crop failures and not enough land were among the immigrants who arrived at Ellis Island. To Angel Island on the West Coast came young men from farm villages in southern China. They had heard about the discovery of gold in California in 1849, and they wanted to earn money for their families at home.

Today laws limit the number of people who can immigrate to the United States each year. But in special cases, Congress has granted entry to people escaping war and persecution. In recent years, the largest numbers of immigrants have come from Latin America, Asia, and Africa.

Less than one percent of the people who live in the United States today have Native American **ancestors**. All the others are immigrants or descendants of immigrants from every nation in the world.

Use information in the reading on pages 60 and 61 to complete the sentences. Underline or highlight the sentence in the reading that supports your answer. Then write the sentence in the space below the choices.

1. The First Amendment to the Constitution
   a. limits people's rights.
   b. protects people's rights.
   c. violates people's rights.

*Many personal freedoms guaranteed by the Constitution are found in the words of the First Amendment.*

2. Many of the first European immigrants to the United States wanted to
   a. own their own land.
   b. find gold.
   c. work on the railroads.

3. In the 1700s, immigrants to the United States found
   a. more religious tolerance.
   b. many Chinese settlers.
   c. few opportunities.

4. Today laws in the United States
   a. discriminate against European immigrants.
   b. control the number of immigrants.
   c. allow only refugees to immigrate.

**Complete the sentences. Use your own words.**

1. The First Amendment says that _____

   _____

2. Walt Whitman called the United States "a nation of nations" because _____

   _____

**Think about the questions. Share your answers with someone.**

1. How did the desire to escape religious persecution influence immigration to the United States?

2. How does immigration influence the way of life in the United States?

# Pick Your Project

**Do one or more of the following activities. Share your work with someone.**

## Community Matters: Interact!

Talk to at least three immigrants from different home countries and ask their reasons for coming to the United States. List each person's reasons. How are they similar? How are they different?

## In the News: Get the Facts!

Read, watch, and listen to the same news story as it is reported in newspapers and on TV, radio, and the Internet. Make a chart like the one below to compare the news sources.

*Subject of news story:* _____

| Source | How report differs from others? | Was it easy to understand? | Was it objective? | Was it comprehensive? |
|---|---|---|---|---|
| **Newspaper** | | | | |
| **News magazine** | | | | |
| **TV or radio station** | | | | |
| **Internet website** | | | | |

Compare the news sources. Which was easiest to understand? Which was most objective? Which was most comprehensive? Are some media better for communicating certain types of information? If you could choose only two sources of information, which would you choose? Why?

## Creative Works: React!

Imagine that you are a reporter. You are assigned to attend the Clay Sanford rally at Green Meadow Park and to write a story on the effects of immigration. Use these questions as a guide.

▶ What kind of background research would you do?
▶ What would you look for at the rally?
▶ Would you interview Clay Sanford? If so, what would you ask him?
▶ What other types of people would you interview to balance the story and make it objective? What questions would you ask them?

# Inside Information

## Symbols of a Country

The New York Yankees, Miami Dolphins, Chicago Bulls, Los Angeles Galaxy . . . all sports teams have nicknames and symbols well known to their fans. Businesses use logos and slogans to attract customers. Even countries use symbols that have special meaning.

The Stars and Stripes—the flag of the United States—is the country's most recognizable symbol. But other symbols are also important to people who live in the United States. Some of these are pictured below. Match each one with its description.

3

1. Home of the president of the United States

2. Place where Congress—the Senate and House of Representatives—meets.

3. National bird: the bald eagle

4. Symbol of the Declaration of Independence located in Independence Hall in Philadelphia. Weighs over 2,000 pounds.

5. Located in New York Harbor. Presented to the United States in 1884 by the Franco American Union. Over 300 feet tall.

6. Adopted in 1782. Design represents the authority of Congress and the thirteen original states.

For bonus points, identify the inscriptions, or words, on symbols 4, 5, and 6 by writing the correct number below.

_____ A. *"Proclaim liberty throughout the land unto all the inhabitants thereof."*

_____ B. *"E Pluribus Unum—One Out of Many"*

_____ C. *"Give me your tired, your poor, your huddled masses yearning to breathe free . . ."*

**Now check your progress on Unit 5, *Collision Course, Part 1*. Turn to page 138.**

# 6 Collision Course, Part 2

The First Amendment protects freedom of speech for all people.

*In this episode two lawyers, a father and son, disagree about whether they should represent an anti-immigrant client, whose ideas they oppose.*

*How can lawyers defend a client if they disagree with his ideas?*

# Preview the Story

**Look at the pictures. Think about these questions. Share your ideas with someone.**

What do you see?

What are these people thinking? What are they feeling?

What do you think will happen?

# Preview Turning Points

Freedom of speech is an important right in a representative democracy. But it is not always easy to support this right for people whose ideas are different from our own.

**Think about the ideas above as you look at the pictures.**

**Think about these questions. Share your answers with someone.**

🔔 Which examples of free speech would you find it difficult to support?

🔔🔔 Have you seen someone interfere with another person's right of free speech? What happened?

🔔🔔🔔 Should freedom of speech ever be denied? For what reasons? Who should decide?

# Remember the Story

★ **Read what people said. Look at the pictures. Complete the chart.**

Carla Castillo

Jess Holcomb
City Attorney

Linda Matthews
City employee

Ray Matthews
Unemployed worker

Francisco Lopez
Attorney

Hector Lopez
Attorney

Mayor Reilly

Clay Sanford

TV audience

| *What People Said* | *Who Said It* | *To Whom* |
|---|---|---|
| 1. "We're being manipulated by the bigot." | *Hector Lopez* | *Francisco Lopez* |
| 2. "No one said the Constitution only applies to people we like." | | |
| 3. "I don't think we can afford to do anything that makes us look biased against him." | | |
| 4. "Another rally, another riot. You still think this is all coincidence?" | | |
| 5. "Why did you take him? What were you thinking?" | | |
| 6. "You've never been sympathetic to my situation. I might be better off waiting until your father recovers." | | |
| 7. "And in a dramatic decision, a federal court found the city guilty of violating Clay Sanford's First Amendment rights." | | |

★ ★ **Put the paragraphs in order. Number them 1 to 7.**

_____ a. A few days after the rally, as Francisco and his son leave the courthouse, a man rushes up. He shouts, "You're a <u>traitor</u> to your own kind," and shoots Francisco.

___*1*___ b. Clay Sanford held a rally against immigration, which the police stopped. He claims the city <u>violated</u> his right to free speech. Sanford hires the law firm of Francisco and Hector Lopez to represent him in a lawsuit against the city. Hector says Sanford is a <u>bigot.</u> He refuses to represent him, but his father continues with the case.

_____ c. Diane Clayton asks Linda about Ronnie and tells her that there is a new list of city job openings. Linda says Ray has found part-time work as a machinist in another state and the family will be moving.

_____ d. The court rules the city did violate Mr. Sanford's First Amendment rights. Hector tells reporters that the case "may have been <u>controversial</u> from the public's standpoint, but not from a constitutional one. The court made the right decision."

_____ e. After Francisco is hospitalized, Hector takes the case. He's concerned that if he doesn't, Sanford will use a <u>continuance</u> to get more publicity. He has also learned how important it is to protect free speech. His father was shot by a man who didn't like what his father was saying.

_____ f. Even though he has filed a lawsuit against the city, Sanford requests police protection at his next rally. The mayor *is* worried about looking <u>biased</u> against Sanford. The police chief agrees to have police at the rally. But even with the police there, what begins as a small disturbance becomes a riot. Linda and Ray's son Ronnie is hurt.

**Write the underlined words in the paragraphs next to their definitions below.**

1. acted against the law _____

2. preferring one person or group over another _____

3. person with extreme opinions about race, religion, or politics _____

4. someone disloyal to his or her country or friends _____ *traitor* _____

5. postponement of a hearing or trial _____

6. causing disagreement because people have strong opinions about it _____

🔔 🔔 🔔 **Imagine that Clay Sanford talks to Hector Lopez. Role-play with someone. Your partner is Clay Sanford. You are Hector Lopez.**

When will your father be back at work?

When he has fully recovered.

CLAY SANFORD: Well, you won the case. How do you feel?

HECTOR LOPEZ:

CLAY SANFORD: Why do you think the city will lose an appeal?

HECTOR LOPEZ:

CLAY SANFORD: You know I'll continue to exercise my right to free speech.

HECTOR LOPEZ:

*Collision Course, Part 2* **69**

# Remember Turning Points

🔔 **Decide whether the activities listed below are protected by the First Amendment. Write the correct letter on the line.**

a. protected by the
First Amendment

b. never protected or allowed because activity presents "clear and present danger" to others

__a__ 1. a parade by members and supporters of the Nazi Party

_____ 2. protest march by farm workers

_____ 3. civil rights march on Washington

_____ 4. Native Americans's "longest walk" protest against unfair treatment

_____ 5. protest march against the Vietnam War

_____ 6. demonstration against nuclear weapons

🔔🔔 **Put the items in the box in order. Check each one after you use it.**

| |
|---|
| • Nazis apply for parade permit |
| • American Nazi Party takes case to court |
| • City passes laws to stop parade |
| • First Amendment not for people who want to destroy freedom |
| • Jewish survivors of Nazi concentration camps settle in Skokie ✓ |
| • First Amendment for everyone |
| • Supreme Court rules in favor of Nazi Party |

1. **Jewish survivors of Nazi concentration camps settle in Skokie**

↓

2.

↓

3.

↓

4.

↙ ↘

5. Nazi Party argues that

6. City argues that

↙ ↘

7.

**Based on this episode and on your own experience, write reasons to restrict and reasons not to restrict freedom of speech.**

| Freedom of Speech | |
|---|---|
| Reasons to Restrict | Reasons not to Restrict |
| *The country would be protected from people opposed to the government.* | *A country cannot progress without the free flow of ideas.* |
| | |
| | |

# Making Connections

**Read the quote below. Think about the questions. Share your answers with someone.**

> The First Amendment protects the expression of all ideas.

1. In this story, who claims the city is violating his constitutional right to freedom of speech?

2. Who disagrees with the client's ideas, but is still willing to defend the client's rights?

3. Who has trouble distinguishing between what a person says and his constitutional right to say it?

1. What happens that causes the change of lawyers in the case?

2. What is the decision in the case?

1. Why do the father and son disagree about taking the case?

2. Why does the son change his opinion?

3. How would other decisions or actions have made a difference?

> I may disapprove of what you say, but I will defend to
> the death your right to say it.
> —Voltaire

## Why did the Founders value freedom of speech?

It is not easy for people to tolerate ideas that are very different from their own, especially when those ideas hurt the dignity and feelings of others in the community. But to the **Founders** of the United States, freedom of speech and expression were of great importance.

The Founders knew that throughout history, governments had tried to stop people from criticizing government actions and promoting new ideas. In the colonies, people had suffered—and some had died—for saying what they thought. In 1660 in the Massachusetts Colony, a woman named Mary Dyer taught that all men and women were equal before God, and that slavery, war, and capital punishment were evil. The **Puritans** hanged Mary Dyer because her ideas were different from theirs.

A government that controls what people say also decides which beliefs and opinions are acceptable. The Founders did not think that this was the role of government. They did not want government to spy on individuals or groups with opinions they considered dangerous. Thus, the only way to protect freedom of speech was to protect it for all people, no matter how disagreeable their ideas might be.

## What are the benefits of freedom of speech?

The Founders also believed that an individual's right to express beliefs was essential in a **representative democracy**. They knew that people could not make wise choices about candidates for public office without good information. Freedom of speech does not guarantee "good information," but it does increase the chances of people getting it.

There are other arguments for the importance of free speech.

▶ Freedom of speech allows people to influence public opinion and achieve peaceful social change over time, without resorting to violence.
▶ The freedom to say what you think and to hear other points of view promotes personal growth and human dignity.
▶ People can develop new ideas and make good decisions when there is a free exchange of facts and ideas. This helps to increase knowledge and awareness.

### When is it difficult to maintain the commitment to free speech?

At times in U.S. history, people have tried to **repress** disturbing ideas. This often occurred during times of war or when people and government felt threatened. In 1901, an **anarchist** killed President William McKinley. Many states reacted by making it a crime to urge the overthrow of government by force.

When the United States entered World War I, people felt the nation needed to be protected from people who promoted resistance to the country or the war effort. The federal government and thirty three states passed laws making it illegal to promote **rebellion** against the United States. For several decades, federal and state governments prosecuted people who argued for **draft resistance**, mass **strikes**, or the overthrow of government.

For example, in 1949, just after World War II, eleven **communist** leaders were convicted of working for the violent overthrow of the U.S. government. They appealed their conviction to the Supreme Court claiming that their freedom of speech had been denied. In 1951, by a 6–2 vote, the Court rejected their appeal. The Chief Justice said that the actions of the eleven presented a "clear and present danger" to the nation, and that they should be punished. Judge Hugo Black disagreed with the majority, saying:

> There is hope that in calmer times this or some later court will restore the First Amendment liberties to the . . . place where they belong in a free society.

This chapter in U.S. history is a reminder of how difficult it can be to maintain the freedoms that are important to a democratic nation.

### Should free speech ever be limited?

Sometimes it may be fair to limit the right of free speech to protect other rights. As an example, should a person have the right to yell "Fire!" in a crowded theater just to frighten people, even though there is no fire? Why is this not considered a right of free speech? What if someone wants to convince people to change the country's form of

government? Should the government be able to keep that person from doing this? What if an unpopular group wants to have a public demonstration? Should the government be able to stop the group just because the demonstration may cause a riot?

Over the years, the courts have developed guidelines to help them decide when the right to free expression interferes with other important rights and interests. When freedom of expression is dangerous to public safety or **national security**, the courts have sometimes allowed freedom of expression to be limited.

# Find Out More: Key Ideas

🔔 **Use information in the reading on pages 72 and 73 to complete the sentences. Underline or highlight the sentence in the reading that supports your answer. Then write the sentence in the space below the choices.**

1. To protect freedom of speech, everyone must be permitted to express ideas,
   a. even if they offend others.
   b. but not if they offend others.
   c. even if they are dangerous to others.

   *Thus, the only way to protect freedom of speech was to protect it for all people, no matter how disagreeable their ideas might be.*

2. The right to freedom of speech ensures that
   a. all information is accurate.
   b. all people get information.
   c. more information is available.

   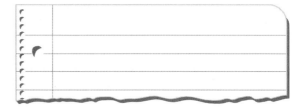

3. After World War I, many states made it a crime to encourage people to
   a. rebel against the government.
   b. support the U.S. war effort.
   c. be critical of the government.

4. The U.S. courts allow freedom of expression to be limited when
   a. the message is unpopular.
   b. many people's feelings may be hurt.
   c. the information puts people in great danger.

🔔🔔 **Complete the sentences. Use your own words.**

1. The Founders of the United States thought freedom of speech was important because

   _____

   _____

2. Freedom of speech can help decrease violence because _____

   _____

🔔🔔🔔 **Think about the questions. Share your answers with someone.**

1. What is an example of the U.S. government limiting freedom of speech?

2. How would your life in the United States be different without freedom of speech?

# Pick Your Project

**Do one or more of the following activities. Share your work with someone.**

## Community Matters: Interact!

Contact city hall for information about public demonstrations. Ask these questions. Take notes.

▶ Can anyone plan a demonstration?
▶ What are the requirements to have a parade, rally, or public demonstration?
▶ Is there a fee? If so, what is it?
▶ Are there restrictions?

## In the News: Get the Facts!

The right to freedom of speech is demonstrated daily on talk-radio programs. Listen to several talk shows to discover the kinds of issues discussed and the variety of opinions expressed. Choose one current issue. Write the major ideas on a chart like the one below.

| Program and Date | Issue or Topic | Opinion For | Opinion Against |
|---|---|---|---|
| **Talk it Out WWKK August 9** | **Smoking in restaurants** | **Smoking should be allowed in all restaurants as long as there is a "non-smoking" area.** | **Even with separate areas, smoke will spread to non-smoking sections. Everyone's health is threatened.** |

Evaluate the arguments for and against the issue. Which opinions were supported by facts? Which seemed to be biased? Form your own opinion based on a careful examination of the information.

## Creative Works: React!

Think of an issue that is important to you. Try to convince other people to support your point of view by doing one of the following activities.

▶ Create a poster or billboard.
▶ Write a speech for a rally.
▶ Design a fact sheet.
▶ Create a radio announcement about a rally.

# Inside Information

## Capitol Games

Test yourself about the legislative branch of U.S. government. If you are not sure of an answer, review Units 2 and 4 and the Constitution (see pages 89–107), or ask a friend. Use a coin as a game piece, and move one space each time you answer correctly. Answers are on page 124.

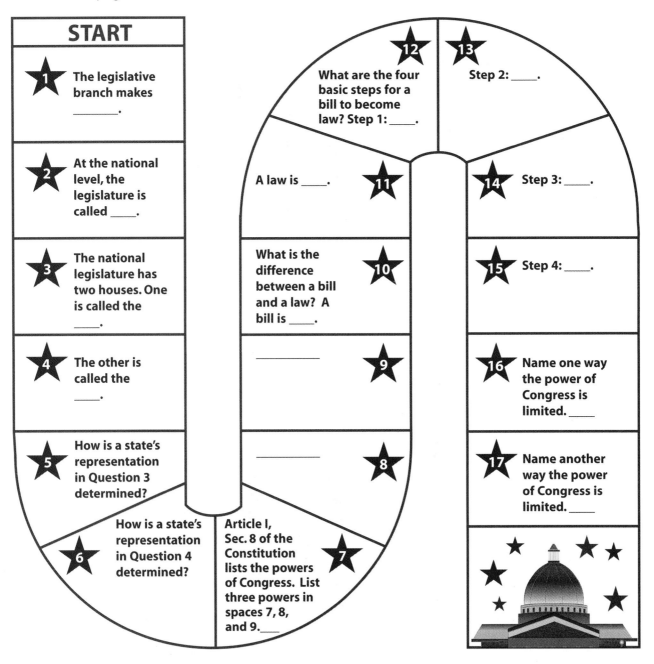

**START**

★ **1** The legislative branch makes _____.

★ **2** At the national level, the legislature is called _____.

★ **3** The national legislature has two houses. One is called the _____.

★ **4** The other is called the _____.

★ **5** How is a state's representation in Question 3 determined?

★ **6** How is a state's representation in Question 4 determined?

★ **7** Article I, Sec. 8 of the Constitution lists the powers of Congress. List three powers in spaces 7, 8, and 9.____

★ **8**

★ **9**

★ **10** What is the difference between a bill and a law? A bill is _____.

★ **11** A law is _____.

★ **12** What are the four basic steps for a bill to become law? Step 1: _____.

★ **13** Step 2: _____.

★ **14** Step 3: _____.

★ **15** Step 4: _____.

★ **16** Name one way the power of Congress is limited. _____

★ **17** Name another way the power of Congress is limited. _____

**Now check your progress on Unit 6, *Collision Course, Part 2.* Turn to page 140.**

# 7 | A Delicate Balance

Top News of the Day
"New Accusations"

The U.S. Constitution protects the freedom of the press—an important right in a democracy.

*In this episode a judge jails reporter Carla Castillo because Carla will not reveal the name of a woman she interviewed.*

*Should a reporter's freedom to report information ever be limited?*

# Preview the Story

**Look at the pictures. Think about these questions. Share your ideas with someone.**

🔔    What do you see?

🔔 🔔    What are these people thinking?  What are they feeling?

🔔 🔔 🔔    What do you think will happen?

# Preview Turning Points

The free exchange of information is essential in a democracy. Freedom of the press is guaranteed in the First Amendment to the Constitution.

**Think about the ideas above as you look at the pictures.**

**Think about these questions. Share your answers with someone.**

🔔 Which pictures represent freedom of the press? Which do not?

🔔🔔 What kinds of stories do you expect to read about when there is a free press?

🔔🔔🔔 What happens when freedom of the press does not exist?

# Remember the Story

Read what people said. Look at the pictures. Complete the chart.

Carla Castillo

Susan Miller

Prosecuting attorneys

Reporters

Steve Richardson
News Producer

Marty Siegel
Assistant District Attorney

Warren Talbot

| What People Said | Who Said It | To Whom |
|---|---|---|
| 1. "This woman's story is a lie from beginning to end." | **Warren Talbot** | **Reporters** |
| 2. "She's got to convince the jury. Otherwise, they'll misinterpret her anxiety and think she's lying." | | |
| 3. "This woman's testimony can establish a pattern. Tell us who she is." | | |
| 4. "I want to see Talbot get what he deserves, but if I give up my source, I'm finished as a reporter." | | |
| 5. "I see a real future here for you." | | |
| 6. "I want to put an end to it. I want to let him know that he can't control my life anymore." | | |

Put the paragraphs in order. Number them 1 to 6.

_____ a. Talbot invites Carla's <u>source</u>, Susan, into his office. His interest in her once again makes her afraid. She quits her job. Then she visits Carla in jail and tells her she will testify against Talbot.

_____ b. The prosecution cannot ask Talbot questions about these new charges unless the woman who made them appears in court. Anything she said to Carla is <u>hearsay</u>. The prosecution asks Carla to tell them the woman's name, but she refuses. If she reveals her source, she says, no one will confide in her again.

_**1**_   c. Warren Talbot, a well-known business leader, is on trial for raping an employee. Carla Castillo asks Talbot if he is negotiating an <u>out-of-court settlement</u>. His lawyer says Talbot is innocent and doesn't need to negotiate anything.

_____ d. Carla receives a <u>subpoena</u> to appear in court. The prosecuting attorneys request that she reveal her source. The judge starts to deny the request because of First Amendment protections. But then the defense attorney also demands to know the name of the source so he can question her in court. Mr. Talbot, he says, is suing *Metro 5 News* for <u>slander</u>.

_____ e. Carla receives an <u>anonymous</u> call from a woman who says that she also was raped by Talbot. The caller agrees to meet Carla if she promises not to reveal her identity. Carla reports her story on *Metro 5 News*, without revealing the woman's name.

_____ f. Because both attorneys request the woman's name, the judge asks Carla to reveal her source. She refuses. He warns her that she could be charged with <u>contempt of court</u> and jailed. When she again refuses, she is jailed.

**Write the underlined words in the paragraphs next to their definitions below.**

1. not named, person whose name is withheld   _____

2. person who gives information   _____ *source* _____

3. act of disobeying a court order   _____

4. false statements that hurt a person's reputation   _____

5. written legal order that directs a person to appear in court to give testimony   _____

6. something heard, but not known to be true   _____

7. agreement reached outside a court of law   _____

🔔 🔔 🔔   **Imagine that Carla Castillo is the guest on a radio show. Role-play with someone. Your partner is the caller. You are Carla.**

*Why are you in jail?*

*For not revealing my source for the Talbot case.*

CALLER: Your source can testify against Talbot. Why won't you reveal her identity?

CARLA:

CALLER: You made accusations against Mr. Talbot without revealing a source. How do we know they're true?

CARLA:

CALLER: Was putting you in jail fair?

CARLA:

# Remember Turning Points

Write **T (True) or F (False) next to each statement.**

_T_ 1. From the time the printing press was invented, governments have tried to control what journalists write.

_T_ 2. Totalitarian governments censor the press more than democratic governments.

_F_ 3. The British government successfully controlled the press in the American colonies.

_T_ 4. The people's right to know what is happening was so important to the Founders of the United States that they included freedom of the press in the First Amendment to the Constitution.

_F_ 5. There are no limits to freedom of the press in the United States.

**Read each sentence in the box. Write the number of the sentence in the correct space. Put a check next to each sentence after you use it.**

In a Totalitarian Government — 1, 3, 5

In a Democracy — 2, 4, 6

1. People have little or no political power. ✔
2. People have a legal right to know what is happening.
3. The government controls what reporters write.
4. Reporters do not have the right to report information that they know is false.
5. Newspapers do not print articles that criticize the government.
6. Reporters do not have the right to write articles that put others in danger.

**Freedom of the press involves rights and responsibilities. For each right or responsibility below, give an example from the story or from real life.**

| Freedom of the Press | |
|---|---|
| Right or Responsibility | Example |
| 1. People in a community have the right to know. | *what their city council is doing* |
| 2. Reporters have the responsibility to print the truth. | |
| 3. Reporters have the responsibility not to publish articles that cause danger to others. | |
| 4. Reporters have the responsibility not to publish information that they know is false. | |

## Making Connections

**Read the quote below. Think about the questions. Share your answers with someone.**

> As with any other right, there are limits to freedom of the press.

1. In this story, who represents "the press"?
2. How is freedom of the press challenged?

1. How did the assistant district attorney's office try to limit freedom of the press?

1. What did Carla and *Metro 5 News* do?
2. What else could they have done?

Since the invention of the printing press, governments have tried to prevent the publication of information that criticizes the government and its leaders. Controlling the press is a way to control the thoughts and minds of the people.

**What were some challenges to the press during colonial times?**

In the Virginia Colony in 1682, John Buckner was **accused** of printing the laws so people would know what they were. Unfortunately, he did this without permission of the governor! As a result, the English governor outlawed all printing presses in the colony. He said that printed words encouraged people to learn, and to criticize their government. It was his hope that God would save Virginia from free schools and printing presses for at least one hundred years!

The first newspapers in the colonies appeared in the early 1700s. At that time, the colonies were ruled by England and governed by its laws. Although there was limited freedom of the press in England, it was not allowed in the colonies. For this reason, **underground newspapers** provided important information for the colonists.

In 1735, John Peter Zenger, publisher of the *Weekly Journal* in the colony of New York, accused the governor of accepting bribes and interfering with elections. The governor had copies of the newspaper burned, and he had Zenger arrested. He accused Zenger of trying to start a rebellion against the government.

Zenger's lawyer argued that his client was **innocent** because he wrote the truth. He said that freedom of the press is a basic right of the people. After a long trial, the jury decided that Zenger had published the truth about the governor. They found

Zenger not guilty and released him from jail.

The result of this trial did not change English law, nor did it guarantee the freedom of the press in the colonies. But it did inspire other colonists to continue the fight for freedom of the press.

Even after the colonies became independent and freedom of the press was established, some state governments accused editors of printing criticisms of the government. This was particularly true before the Civil War. Before the war began in 1860, several states passed laws saying it was a crime to print articles against slavery. Only after World War I did the Supreme Court expand protection of freedom of the press.

## What is the role of the press today?

The word "press" now includes more than the newspapers, pamphlets, and public notices used two hundred years ago. It also refers to radio and television news reports and communications by computer. The **free exchange of ideas** in a democracy is still as important.

Under the U.S. Constitution, the people give government its authority. This means that government is the servant, not the master, of the people. Citizens have the right to tell officials in the government what to do and how to do it. They also have the right to know how government is performing.

The First Amendment protects this **"right to know."** The press has the right to report about government actions and the work of government officials. It does not have the right to report information that is false, or only partly true. Members of the press are responsible for checking their stories and reporting only the facts.

Sometimes the people's right to know and the government's responsibility for national security are in conflict. When the nation is at war, government may try to control the release of information that could **endanger** the U.S. military or the country in general. Some people say that controlling information is never right. Most people agree that it may be necessary in special situations, but that control of the press must never be used to hide information people have the right to know.

Use information in the reading on pages 84 and 85 to complete the sentences. Underline or highlight the sentence in the reading that supports your answer. Then write the sentence in the space below the choices.

1. In the 1680s, the governor of the Virginia colony
   a. decided to tax all printing presses.
   b. made it illegal to have a printing press.
   c. gave John Buckner a printing press.

   *As a result, the English governor outlawed all printing presses in the colony.*

2. In 1735, a jury found John Peter Zenger not guilty because he
   a. printed the truth.
   b. didn't know the law.
   c. started a rebellion.

3. The press in the United States is free to
   a. print partially true information.
   b. distribute false information.
   c. investigate the president's actions.

4. The U.S. government may limit freedom of the press in order to
   a. stop criticism of the government.
   b. protect U.S. troops during a war.
   c. control public opinion.

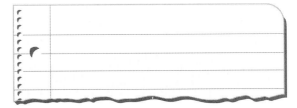

Complete the sentences. Use your own words.

1. The governor of Virginia didn't like printing presses because _____

2. The trial of John Peter Zenger was important because _____

Think about the questions. Share your answers with someone.

1. How does a free press make a government more responsible to the people?

2. How does freedom of the press affect you?

# Pick Your Project

Do one or more of the following activities. Share your work with someone.

## Community Matters: Interact!

Contact the news department of a local radio or television station or local newspaper. Ask to speak to one or two reporters. Ask these questions and take notes.

- ▶ How much do you research a story before you write it or prepare it for broadcast?
- ▶ Do you usually have enough time to check all the facts? If not, how do you decide what to include in your report and what to leave out?
- ▶ How do you feel about using anonymous sources in your stories?
- ▶ Should there be any limits on the press?

## In the News: Get the Facts!

Investigate a news story that is currently in the headlines. Read accounts of the story in three major newspapers. Most libraries will have copies of newspapers for you to read. Make a chart like the one below.

Subject: ***Bombing of U.S. Embassy***

| Source | How were facts reported? Was there enough information? | Is the report accurate? Is the report objective? |
|---|---|---|
| **World Journal** | **Emotional comments by people who were on the scene. Accounts added human interest, but few facts. Little information at this point.** | **Writers seemed to be looking for someone to blame. Not sure conclusions are accurate.** |

Compare and contrast the three accounts of the event. Which resource did you find most valid and complete? Why? What conclusions can you draw about the importance of careful research and objective analysis in reporting the news?

## Creative Works: React!

Write an article about a local event—for example, an accident or a fire. In your article, answer the typical journalist's questions—who, what, when, where, why, and how did the event happen. When you finish your story, think about the experience. Was it easy to get the facts? Did you hear different opinions? How did you decide which was the more accurate point of view, or did you report both in your story?

# Inside Information

## Executive Power

**Complete the sentences. Fill in the puzzle. Get help if you don't know some answers.**

### ACROSS

1. The executive branch enforces _Laws_ passed by Congress.

3. The president is assisted by advisors called the _Congress_.

6. If a president is in favor of a bill passed by Congress, he or she will _Sign_ it.

7. The president gives a _____ of the (12 across) speech at the beginning of each year.

11. The president is the commander-in-_chief_ of the armed forces.

12. The president gives a (7 across) of the _____ speech at the beginning of each year.

14. The president can _veto_ a bill he or she disagrees with.

15. The president can serve _two_ terms in office.

### DOWN

2. The _____ must approve the people the president names to important jobs.

3. The president appoints justices of the Supreme _____.

4. The president can either sign or veto a _____ passed by Congress

5. The president has the power to make an agreement or a _____ with another nation.

8. The president leads the _executive_ branch of government.

9. The president has the power to _____ people to executive and judicial jobs.

10. The president lives in the _____ House.

13. The president is elected for a _four_-year term.

14. If the president dies while in office, the _vice_ president takes over.

**Now check your progress on Unit 7, *A Delicate Balance*.  Turn to page 142.**

## PREAMBLE

We the People of the United States, in Order to form a more perfect Union, establish Justice, insure domestic Tranquility, provide for the common defence, promote the general Welfare, and secure the Blessings of Liberty to ourselves and our Posterity, do ordain and establish this Constitution for the United States of America.

## ARTICLE I

### Section I

All legislative Powers herein granted shall be vested in a Congress of the United States, which shall consist of a Senate and House of Representatives.

### Section 2

1.  The House of Representatives shall be composed of Members chosen every second Year by the People of the several States, and the Electors in each State shall have the Qualifications requisite for Electors of the most numerous Branch of the State Legislature.

2.  No Person shall be a Representative who shall not have attained to the Age of twenty five Years, and been seven Years a Citizen of the United States, and who shall not, when elected, be an Inhabitant of that State in which he shall be chosen.

3.  [Representatives and direct Taxes shall be apportioned among the several States which may be included within this Union, according to their respective Numbers, which shall be determined by adding to the whole Number of free Persons, including those bound to Service for a Term of Years, and excluding Indians not taxed, three fifths of all other Persons.][1] The actual Enumeration shall be made within three Years after the first Meeting of the Congress of the United States, and within every subsequent Term of ten Years, in such Manner as they shall by Law direct. The number of Representatives shall not exceed one for every thirty Thousand, but each State shall have at Least one Representative; and until such enumeration shall be made, the State of New Hampshire shall be entitled to choose three, Massachusetts eight, Rhode-Island and Providence Plantations one, Connecticut five, New York six, New Jersey four, Pennsylvania eight, Delaware one, Maryland six, Virginia ten, North Carolina five, South Carolina five, and Georgia three.

4.  When vacancies happen in the Representation from any State, the Executive Authority thereof shall issue Writs of Election to fill such Vacancies.

5.  The House of Representatives shall choose their Speaker and other Officers; and shall have the sole Power of Impeachment.

---

[1] (Throughout the Constitution, passages enclosed in brackets and marked with footnote numbers have been changed by amendment, as indicated.) Changed by Section 2 of the Fourteenth Amendment.

## Section 3

1. The Senate of the United States shall be composed of two Senators from each State, [chosen by the Legislature thereof,]$^2$ for six Years; and each Senator shall have one Vote.

2. Immediately after they shall be assembled in consequence of the first Election, they shall be divided as equally as may be into three Classes. The Seats of the Senators of the first Class shall be vacated at the Expiration of the second Year, of the second Class at the Expiration of the fourth Year, and of the third Class at the Expiration of the sixth Year, so that one third may be chosen every second Year; [and if Vacancies happen by Resignation, or otherwise, during the Recess of the Legislature of any State, the Executive thereof may make temporary Appointments until the next Meeting of the Legislature, which shall then fill such Vacancies.]$^3$

3. No Person shall be a Senator who shall not have attained to the Age of thirty Years, and been nine Years a Citizen of the United States, and who shall not, when elected, be an inhabitant of that State for which he shall be chosen.

4. The Vice President of the United States shall be President of the Senate, but shall have no vote, unless they be equally divided.

5. The Senate shall choose their other Officers, and also a President pro tempore, in the Absence of the Vice President, or when he shall exercise the Office of President of the United States.

6. The Senate shall have the sole Power to try all Impeachments. When sitting for that Purpose, they shall be on Oath or Affirmation. When the President of the United States is tried, the Chief Justice shall preside; and no Person shall be convicted without the Concurrence of two thirds of the Members present.

7. Judgment in Cases of Impeachment shall not extend further than to removal from Office, and disqualification to hold and enjoy any Office of Honor, Trust or Profit under the United States; but the Party convicted shall nevertheless be liable and subject to Indictment, Trial, Judgment and Punishment, according to Law.

## Section 4

1. The Times, Places and Manner of holding Elections for Senators and Representatives shall be prescribed in each State by the legislature thereof, but the Congress may at any time by Law make or alter such Regulations, except as to the Places of choosing Senators.

2. The Congress shall assemble at least once in every Year, and such Meeting shall be [on the first Monday in December,]$^4$ unless they shall by Law appoint a different Day.

## Section 5

1. Each House shall be the Judge of the Elections, Returns and Qualifications of its own Members, and a Majority of each shall constitute a Quorum to do Business; but a smaller Number may adjourn from day to day, and may be authorized to compel the Attendance of absent Members, in such Manner, and under such Penalties as each House may provide.

---

$^2$ Changed by the Seventeenth Amendment.
$^3$ Changed by the Seventeenth Amendment.
$^4$ Changed by Section 2 of the Twentieth Amendment.

2. Each House may determine the Rules of its Proceedings, punish its Members for disorderly Behavior, and, with the Concurrence of two thirds, expel a Member.

3. Each House shall keep a journal of its Proceedings, and from time to time publish the same, excepting such Parts as may in their Judgment require Secrecy; and the Yeas and Nays of the Members of either House on any question shall, at the Desire of one fifth of those Present, be entered on the Journal.

4. Neither House, during the Session of Congress, shall, without the Consent of the other, adjourn for more than three days, nor to any other Place than that in which the two Houses shall be sitting.

## Section 6

1. The Senators and Representatives shall receive a Compensation for their Services, to be ascertained by Law, and paid out of the Treasury of the United States. They shall in all Cases, except Treason, Felony, and Breach of the Peace be privileged from Arrest during their Attendance at the Session of their respective Houses, and in going to and returning from the same; and for any Speech or Debate in either House, they shall not be questioned in any other Place.

2. No Senator or Representative shall, during the Time for which he was elected, be appointed to any civil Office under the Authority of the United States, which shall have been created, or the Emoluments whereof shall have been increased during such time; and no Person holding any Office under the United States, shall be a Member of either House during his continuance in Office.

## Section 7

1. All Bills for raising Revenue shall originate in the House of Representatives; but the Senate may propose or concur with Amendments as on other Bills.

2. Every Bill which shall have passed the House of Representatives and the Senate, shall, before it becomes a Law, be presented to the President of the United States; if he approves he shall sign it, but if not he shall return it, with his Objections, to that House in which it shall have originated, who shall enter the Objections at large on their Journal, and proceed to Reconsider it. If after such reconsideration two thirds of that House shall agree to pass the Bill, it shall be sent, together with the Objections, to the other House, by which it shall likewise be reconsidered, and if approved by two thirds of that House, it shall become a Law. But in all such cases the votes of both Houses shall be determined by Yeas and Nays, and the Names of the Persons voting for and against the Bill shall be entered on the Journal of each House respectively. If any Bill shall not be returned by the President within ten Days (Sundays excepted) after it shall have been presented to him, the Same shall be a Law, in like Manner as if he had signed it, unless the Congress by their Adjournment prevent its Return, in which Case it shall not be a Law.

3. Every Order, Resolution, or Vote to which the Concurrence of the Senate and House of Representatives may be necessary (except on a question of Adjournment) shall be presented to the President of the United States; and before the Same shall take Effect, shall be approved by him, or being disapproved by him, shall be repassed by two thirds of the Senate and House of Representatives, according to the Rules and Limitations prescribed in the Case of a Bill.

## Section 8

The Congress shall have power:

1. To lay and collect Taxes, Duties, Imposts and Excises, to pay the Debts and provide for the common Defence and general Welfare of the United States; but all duties, imposts and excises shall be uniform throughout the United States;

2. To borrow Money on the credit of the United States;

3. To regulate Commerce with foreign Nations, and among the several States, and with the Indian Tribes;

4. To establish a uniform Rule of Naturalization, and uniform Laws on the subject of Bankruptcies throughout the United States;

5. To coin Money, regulate the Value thereof, and of foreign Coin, and fix the Standard of Weights and Measures;

6. To provide for the Punishment of counterfeiting the Securities and current Coin of the United States;

7. To establish Post Offices and post Roads;

8. To promote the Progress of Science and useful Arts, by securing for limited Times to Authors and Inventors the exclusive Right to their respective Writings and Discoveries;

9. To constitute Tribunals inferior to the Supreme Court;

10. To define and punish Piracies and Felonies committed on the high Seas, and Offenses against the Law of Nations;

11. To declare War, grant Letters of Marque and Reprisal, and make Rules concerning Captures on Land and Water;

12. To raise and support Armies, but no Appropriation of Money to that Use shall be for a longer Term than two Years;

13. To provide and maintain a Navy;

14. To make Rules for the Government and Regulation of the land and naval Forces;

15. To provide for calling forth the Militia to execute the Laws of the Union, suppress Insurrections and repel Invasions;

16. To provide for organizing, arming, and disciplining the Militia, and for governing such Part of them as may be employed in the Service of the United States, reserving to the States respectively, the Appointment of the Officers, and the Authority of training the Militia according to the discipline prescribed by Congress;

17. To exercise exclusive Legislation in all Cases whatsoever, over such District (not exceeding ten Miles square) as may, by Session of particular States, and the Acceptance of Congress, become the Seat of the Government of the United States, and to exercise like Authority over all Places purchased by the Consent of the Legislature of the State in which the Same shall be, for the Erection of Forts, Magazines, Arsenals, dock-Yards and other needful Buildings; and

18. To make all Laws which shall be necessary and proper for carrying into Execution the foregoing Powers, and all other Powers vested by this Constitution in the Government of the United States, or in any Department or Officer thereof.

## Section 9

1. The Migration or Importation of such Persons as any of the States now existing shall think proper to admit, shall not be prohibited by the Congress prior to the Year one thousand eight hundred and eight, but a Tax or duty may be imposed on such Importation, not exceeding ten dollars for each Person.

2. The Privilege of the Writ of Habeas Corpus shall not be suspended, unless when in Cases of Rebellion or Invasion the public Safety may require it.

3. No Bill of Attainder or ex post facto Law shall be passed.

4. [No Capitation, or other direct, Tax shall be laid, unless in Proportion to the Census or Enumeration herein before directed to be taken.][5]

5. No Tax or Duty shall be laid on Articles exported from any State.

6. No Preference shall be given by any Regulation of Commerce or Revenue to the Ports of one State over those of another; nor shall Vessels bound to, or from, one State, be obliged to enter, clear, or pay Duties in another.

7. No Money shall be drawn from the Treasury, but in Consequence of Appropriations made by Law; and a regular Statement and Account of the Receipts and Expenditures of all public Money shall be published from time to time.

8. No Title of Nobility shall be granted by the United States: And no Person holding any Office of Profit or Trust under them, shall, without the Consent of the Congress, accept of any present, Emolument, Office, or Title, of any kind whatever, from any King, Prince, or foreign State.

## Section 10

1. No State shall enter into any Treaty, Alliance, or Confederation; grant Letters of Marque and Reprisal; coin Money; emit Bills of Credit; make any Thing but gold and silver Coin a Tender in Payment of Debts; pass any Bill of Attainder, ex post facto Law, or Law impairing the Obligation of Contracts, or grant any Title of Nobility.

2. No State shall, without the Consent of the Congress, lay any Imposts or Duties on Imports or Exports, except what may be absolutely necessary for executing its inspection Laws: and the net Produce of all Duties and Imposts, laid by any State on Imports or Exports, shall be for the Use of the Treasury of the United States; and all such Laws shall be subject to the Revision and Control of the Congress.

3. No State shall, without the Consent of Congress, lay any Duty of Tonnage, keep Troops, or Ships of War in time of Peace, enter into any Agreement or Compact with another State, or with a foreign Power, or engage in War, unless actually invaded, or in such imminent Danger as will not admit of delay.

---

[5] Changed by the Sixteenth Amendment.

# ARTICLE II

## Section I

1.  The executive Power shall be vested in a President of the United States of America. He shall hold his Office during the Term of four Years, and, together with the Vice President, chosen for the same Term, be elected, as follows.

2.  Each State shall appoint, in such Manner as the Legislature thereof may direct, a Number of Electors, equal to the whole Number of Senators and Representatives to which the State may be entitled in the Congress: but no Senator or Representative, or Person holding an Office of Trust or Profit under the United States, shall be appointed an Elector.

3.  [The Electors shall meet in their respective states, and vote by Ballot for two Persons, of whom one at least shall not be an Inhabitant of the same State with themselves. And they shall make a List of all the Persons voted for, and of the Number of Votes for each; which List they shall sign and certify, and transmit sealed to the Seat of the Government of the United States, directed to the President of the Senate. The President of the Senate shall, in the Presence of the Senate and House of Representatives, open all the Certificates, and the Votes shall then be counted. The Person having the greatest Number of Votes shall be the President, if such Number be a Majority of the whole Number of Electors appointed; and if there be more than one who have such Majority, and have an equal Number of Votes, then the

    House of Representatives shall immediately choose by Ballot one of them for President; and if no Person have a Majority, then from the five highest on the List the said House shall in like manner choose the President. But in choosing the President, the Votes shall be taken by States, the Representation from each State having one Vote; A quorum for this Purpose shall consist of a Member or Members from two thirds of the States, and a Majority of all the States shall be necessary to a Choice. In every Case, after the Choice of the President, the Person having the greatest Number of Votes of the Electors shall be the Vice President. But if there should remain two or more who have equal Votes, the Senate shall choose from them by Ballot the Vice President.][6]

4.  The Congress may determine the Time of choosing the Electors, and the day on which they shall give their Votes; which Day shall be the same throughout the United States.

5.  No Person except a natural born Citizen, or a Citizen of the United States at the time of the Adoption of this Constitution, shall be eligible to the Office of the President; neither shall any person be eligible to that Office who shall not have attained to the Age of thirty five Years, and been fourteen Years a Resident within the United States.

6.  [In Case of the Removal of the President from Office, or of his Death, Resignation, or Inability to discharge the Powers and Duties of the said Office, the Same shall devolve on the Vice President, and the Congress may by Law provide for the Case of Removal, Death, Resignation or Inability, both of the President and Vice President, declaring what Officer shall then act as President, and such Officer shall act accordingly, until the Disability be removed, or a President shall be elected.][7]

---

[6] Changed by the Twelfth Amendment.
[7] Changed by the Twenty-fifth Amendment.

7. The President shall, at stated Times, receive for his Services, a Compensation, which shall neither be increased nor diminished during the Period for which he shall have been elected, and he shall not receive within that Period any other Emolument from the United States, or any of them.

8. Before he enter the Execution of his Office, he shall take the following Oath or Affirmation:—"I do solemnly swear (or affirm) that I will faithfully execute the Office of President of the United States, and will to the best of my ability, preserve, protect, and defend the Constitution of the United States."

## Section 2

1. The President shall be Commander in Chief of the Army and Navy of the United States, and of the Militia of the several States, when called into the actual Service of the United States; he may require the Opinion, in writing, of the principal Officer in each of the executive Departments, upon any Subject relating to the Duties of their respective Offices, and he shall have Power to grant Reprieves and Pardons for Offenses against the United States, except in Cases of Impeachment.

2. He shall have Power, by and with the Advice and Consent of the Senate, to make Treaties, provided two thirds of the Senators present concur; and he shall nominate, and by and with the Advice and Consent of the Senate, shall appoint Ambassadors, other public Ministers and Consuls, Judges of the supreme Court, and all other Officers of the United States, whose Appointments are not herein otherwise provided for, and which shall be established by Law; but the Congress may by Law vest the Appointment of such inferior Officers, as they think proper, in the President alone, in the Courts of Law, or in the Heads of Departments.

3. The President shall have Power to fill up all Vacancies that may happen during the Recess of the Senate, by granting Commissions which shall expire at the End of their next Session.

## Section 3

He shall from time to time give to the Congress Information of the State of the Union, and recommend to their Consideration such Measures as he shall judge necessary and expedient; he may, on extraordinary Occasions, convene both Houses, or either of them, and in Case of Disagreement between them, with Respect to the Time of Adjournment, he may adjourn them to such Time as he shall think proper; he shall receive Ambassadors and other public Ministers; he shall take Care that the Laws be faithfully executed, and shall Commission all the Officers of the United States.

## Section 4

The President, Vice President and all civil Officers of the United States, shall be removed from Office on Impeachment for, and Conviction of, Treason, Bribery, or other high Crimes and Misdemeanors.

## ARTICLE III

## Section I

The judicial Power of the United States, shall be vested in one supreme Court, and in such inferior Courts as the Congress may from time to time ordain and establish. The Judges, both of the supreme and inferior Courts, shall hold their Offices during good Behavior, and shall, at stated Times, receive for their Services a Compensation, which shall not be diminished during their Continuance in Office.

## Section 2

1.  The judicial Power shall extend to all Cases, in Law and Equity, arising under this Constitution, the Laws of the United States, and Treaties made, or which shall be made, under their Authority;—to all Cases affecting Ambassadors, other public Ministers and Consuls;—to all Cases of admiralty and maritime Jurisdiction;—to Controversies to which the United States shall be a Party; to Controversies between two or more States; [between a State and Citizens of another State;] between Citizens of different States; between Citizens of the same State claiming Lands under Grants of different States; [and between a State, or the Citizens thereof, and foreign States, Citizens or Subjects.][8]

2.  In all Cases affecting Ambassadors, other public Ministers and Consuls, and those in which a State shall be Party, the supreme Court shall have original Jurisdiction. In all the other Cases before mentioned, the supreme Court shall have appellate Jurisdiction, both as to Law and Fact, with such Exceptions, and under such Regulations as the Congress shall make.

3.  The Trial of all Crimes, except in Cases of Impeachment, shall be by Jury; and such Trial shall be held in the State where said Crimes shall have been committed; but when not committed within any State, the Trial shall be at such Place or Places as the Congress may by Law have directed.

## Section 3

1.  Treason against the United States shall consist only in levying War against them, or in adhering to their Enemies, giving them Aid and Comfort. No Person shall be convicted of Treason unless on the Testimony of two Witnesses to the same overt Act, or on Confession in open Court.

2.  The Congress shall have Power to declare the Punishment of Treason, but no Attainder of Treason shall work Corruption of Blood, or Forfeiture except during the Life of the Person attainted.

## ARTICLE IV

### Section 1

Full Faith and Credit shall be given in each State to the public Acts, Records, and judicial Proceedings of every other State; And the Congress may by general Laws prescribe the manner in which such Acts, Records and Proceedings shall be proved, and the Effect thereof.

### Section 2

1.  The Citizens of each State shall be entitled to all Privileges and Immunities of Citizens in the several States.

2.  A Person charged in any State with Treason, Felony, or other Crime, who shall flee from Justice, and be found in another State, shall on Demand of the executive Authority of the State from which he fled, be delivered up, to be removed to the State having Jurisdiction of the Crime.

3.  [No person held to Service or Labour in one State, under the Laws thereof, escaping into another, shall, in Consequence of any Law or Regulation therein, be discharged from such Service or

---

[8] Changed by the Eleventh Amendment.

Labour, but shall be delivered up on Claim of the Party to whom such Service or Labour may be due.]9

## Section 3

1. New States may be admitted by the Congress into this Union; but no new State shall be formed or erected within the Jurisdiction of any other State; nor any State be formed by the Junction of two or more States, or parts of States, without the Consent of the Legislatures of the States concerned as well as of the Congress.

2. The Congress shall have Power to dispose of and make all needful Rules and Regulations respecting the territory or other Property belonging to the United States; and nothing in this Constitution shall be so construed as to Prejudice any Claims of the United States, or of any particular State.

## Section 4

The United States shall guarantee to every State in this Union a Republican Form of Government, and shall protect each of them against Invasion; and on Application of the Legislature, or of the Executive (when the Legislature cannot be convened) against domestic Violence.

## ARTICLE V

The Congress, whenever two thirds of both Houses shall deem it necessary, shall propose Amendments to this Constitution, or, on the Application of the Legislatures of two thirds of the several States, shall call a Convention for proposing Amendments, which, in either Case, shall be valid to all Intents and Purposes, as Part of this Constitution, when ratified by the Legislatures of three fourths of the several States, or by Conventions in three fourths thereof, as the one or the other Mode of Ratification may be proposed by the Congress; Provided that no Amendment which may be made prior to the Year One thousand eight hundred and eight shall in any Manner affect the first and fourth Clauses in the Ninth Section of the first Article; and that no State, without its Consent, shall be deprived of its equal Suffrage in the Senate.

## ARTICLE VI

1. All debts contracted and Engagements entered into, before the Adoption of this Constitution, shall be as valid against the United States under this Constitution, as under the Confederation.

2. This Constitution, and the Laws of the United States which shall be made in Pursuance thereof, and all Treaties made, or which shall be made, under the Authority of the United States, shall be the supreme Law of the Land; and the Judges in every State shall be bound thereby, any Thing in the Constitution or Laws of any State to the Contrary notwithstanding.

3. The Senators and Representatives before mentioned, and the Members of the several State Legislatures, and all executive and judicial Officers, both of the United States and of the several States, shall be bound by Oath or Affirmation, to support this Constitution; but no religious Test shall ever be required as a Qualification to any Office or public Trust under the United States.

---

9 Changed by the Thirteenth Amendment.

# ARTICLE VII

The Ratification of the Conventions of nine States, shall be sufficient for the Establishment of this Constitution between the States so ratifying the Same.

Done in Convention by the unanimous consent of the States present the seventeenth day of September in the year of our Lord one thousand seven hundred and eighty seven and of the Independence of the United States of America the Twelfth. In witness whereof we have hereunto subscribed our Names,

George Washington—President
and deputy from Virginia

(This Constitution was adopted on September 17, 1787 by the Constitutional Convention, and was declared ratified on July 2, 1788)

# Signers of the Constitution

**New-Hampshire**
*John Langdon*
*Nicholas Gilman*

**Massachusetts**
*Nathaniel Gorham*
*Rufus King*

**Connecticut**
*William Samuel Johnson*
*Roger Sherman*

**New York**
*Alexander Hamilton*

**New Jersey**
*William Livingston*
*David Brearley*
*William Paterson*
*Jonathan Dayton*

**Pennsylvania**
*Benjamin Franklin*
*Thomas Mifflin*
*Robert Morris*
*George Clymer*
*Thomas Fitzsimons*
*Jared Ingersoll*
*James Wilson*
*Gouverneur Morris*

**Delaware**
*George Read*
*Gunning Bedford, Jr.*
*John Dickinson*
*Richard Bassett*
*Jacob Broom*

**Maryland**
*James McHenry*
*Daniel of St. Tho. Jenifer*
*Daniel Carroll*

**Virginia**
*John Blair*
*James Madison, Junior*

**North Carolina**
*William Blount*
*Richard Dobbs Spaight*
*Hugh Williamson*

**South Carolina**
*John Ruthledge*
*Charles Cotesworth Pinckney*
*Charles Pinckney*
*Pierce Butler*

**Georgia**
*William Few*
*Abraham Baldwin*

*Attest: William Jackson,*
*Secretary*

# AMENDMENTS TO THE CONSTITUTION
## OF THE UNITED STATES OF AMERICA

## AMENDMENT I

Congress shall make no law respecting an establishment of religion, or prohibiting the free exercise thereof, or abridging the freedom of speech, or of the press, or the right of the people peaceably to assemble, and to petition the Government for a redress of grievances. (Ratified December, 1791.)

## AMENDMENT II

A well regulated Militia, being necessary to the security of a free State, the right of the people to keep and bear Arms, shall not be infringed. (Ratified December, 1791.)

## AMENDMENT III

No Soldier shall, in time of peace be quartered in any house, without the consent of the Owner, nor in time of war, but in a manner to be prescribed by law. (Ratified December, 1791.)

## AMENDMENT IV

The right of the people to be secure in their persons, houses, papers, and effects, against unreasonable searches and seizures, shall not be violated, and no Warrants shall issue, but upon probable cause, supported by Oath or affirmation, and particularly describing the place to be searched, and the persons or things to be seized. (Ratified December, 1791.)

## AMENDMENT V

No person shall be held to answer for a capital, or otherwise infamous crime, unless on a presentment or indictment of a Grand Jury, except in cases arising in the land or naval forces, or in the Militia, when in actual service in time of War or public danger; nor shall any person be subject for the same offence to be twice put in jeopardy of life or limb, nor shall be compelled in any criminal case to be a witness against himself, nor be deprived of life, liberty, or property, without due process of law; nor shall private property be taken for public use without just compensation. (Ratified December, 1791.)

## AMENDMENT VI

In all criminal prosecutions, the accused shall enjoy the right to a speedy and public trial, by an impartial jury of the State and district wherein the crime shall have been committed; which district shall have been previously ascertained by law, and to be informed of the nature and cause of the accusation; to be confronted with the witnesses against him; to have compulsory process for obtaining witnesses in his favor, and to have the assistance of counsel for his defence. (Ratified December, 1791.)

## AMENDMENT VII

In Suits at common law, where the value in controversy shall exceed twenty dollars, the right of trial by jury shall be preserved, and no fact tried by a jury shall be otherwise re-examined in any Court of the United States, than according to the rules of the common law. (Ratified December, 1791.)

## AMENDMENT VIII

Excessive bail shall not be required, nor excessive fines imposed, nor cruel and unusual punishments inflicted. (Ratified December, 1791.)

## AMENDMENT IX

The enumeration in the Constitution of certain rights shall not be construed to deny or disparage others retained by the people. (Ratified December, 1791.)

## AMENDMENT X

The powers not delegated to the United States by the Constitution, nor prohibited by it to the States, are reserved to the States respectively, or to the people. (Ratified December, 1791.)

## AMENDMENT XI

The Judicial power of the United States shall not be construed to extend to any suit in law or equity, commenced or prosecuted against one of the United States by Citizens of another State, or by Citizens or Subjects of any Foreign State. (Ratified February, 1795.)

## AMENDMENT XII

The Electors shall meet in their respective states, and vote by ballot for President and Vice President, one of whom, at least, shall not be an inhabitant of the same state with themselves; they shall name in their ballots the person voted for as President, and in distinct ballots the person voted for as Vice-President, and they shall make distinct lists of all persons voted for as President, and of all persons voted for as Vice-President, and of the number of votes for each, which lists they shall sign and certify, and transmit sealed to the seat of the government of the United States, directed to the President of the Senate;—The President of the Senate shall, in the presence of the Senate and House of Representatives, open all the certificates and the votes shall then be counted;—The person having the greatest number of votes for President, shall be the President, if such number be a majority of the whole number of Electors appointed; and if no person have such majority, then from the persons having the highest numbers not exceeding three on the list of those voted for as President, the House of Representatives shall choose immediately, by ballot, the President. But in choosing the President, the votes shall be taken by states, the representation from each state having one vote; a quorum for this purpose shall consist of a member or members from two-thirds of the states, and a majority of all the states shall be necessary to a choice. [And if the House of Representatives shall not choose a President whenever the right of choice shall devolve upon them, before the fourth day of March next following, then the Vice-President shall act as President, as in the case of the death or other constitutional disability of the President—][1] The person having the greatest number of votes as Vice-President, shall be the Vice-President, if such number be a majority of the whole number of Electors appointed, and if no person have a majority, then from the two highest numbers on the list, the Senate shall choose the Vice-President; a quorum for the purpose shall consist of two-thirds of the whole number of Senators, and a majority of the whole number shall be necessary to a choice. But no person constitutionally ineligible to the office of President shall be eligible to that of Vice-President of the United States. (Ratified June, 1804.)

---

[1] Superseded by Section 3 of the Twentieth Amendment.

## AMENDMENT XIII

### Section 1

Neither slavery nor involuntary servitude, except as a punishment for crime whereof the party shall have been duly convicted, shall exist within the United States, or any place subject to their jurisdiction.

### Section 2

Congress shall have power to enforce this article by appropriate legislation. (Ratified December, 1865.)

## AMENDMENT XIV

### Section 1

All persons born or naturalized in the United States and subject to the jurisdiction thereof, are citizens of the United States and of the State wherein they reside. No State shall make or enforce any law which shall abridge the privileges or immunities of citizens of the United States; nor shall any State deprive any person of life, liberty, or property, without due process of law; nor deny to any person within its jurisdiction the equal protection of the laws.

### Section 2

Representatives shall be apportioned among the several States according to their respective numbers, counting the whole number of persons in each State, excluding Indians not taxed. But when the right to vote at any election for the choice of electors for President and Vice President of the United States, Representatives in Congress, the Executive and Judicial officers of a State, or the members of the Legislature thereof, is denied to any of the male inhabitants of such State, being twenty-one years of age, and citizens of the United States, or in any way abridged, except for participation in rebellion, or other crime, the basis of representation therein shall be reduced in the proportion which the number of such male citizens shall bear to the whole number of male citizens twenty-one years of age in such State.

### Section 3

No person shall be a Senator or a Representative in Congress, or elector of President and Vice President, or hold any office, civil or military, under the United States, or under any State, who, having previously taken an oath, as a member of Congress, or as an officer of the United States, or as a member of any State legislature, or as an executive or judicial officer of any State, to support the Constitution of the United States, shall have engaged in insurrection or rebellion against the same, or given aid or comfort to the enemies thereof. But Congress may by a vote of two-thirds of each House, remove such disability.

### Section 4

The validity of the public debt of the United States, authorized by law, including debts incurred for payment of pensions and bounties for services in suppressing insurrection or rebellion, shall not be questioned. But neither the United States nor any State shall assume or pay any debt or obligation incurred in aid of insurrection or rebellion against the United States, or any claim for the loss or emancipation of any slave; but all such debts, obligations and claims shall be held illegal and void.

## Section 5

The Congress shall have power to enforce, by appropriate legislation, the provisions of this article. (Ratified July, 1868.)

## AMENDMENT XV

### Section 1

The right of citizens of the United States to vote shall not be denied or abridged by the United States or by any State on account of race, color, or previous condition of servitude.

### Section 2

The Congress shall have power to enforce this article by appropriate legislation. (Ratified February, 1870.)

## AMENDMENT XVI

The Congress shall have power to lay and collect taxes on incomes, from whatever source derived, without apportionment among the several States, and without regard to any census or enumeration. (Ratified February, 1913.)

## AMENDMENT XVII

The Senate of the United States shall be composed of two Senators from each State, elected by the people thereof, for six years; and each Senator shall have one vote. The electors in each State shall have the qualifications requisite for electors of the most numerous branch of the State legislatures.

When vacancies happen in the representation of any State in the Senate, the executive authority of such State shall issue writs of election to fill such vacancies: Provided, That the legislature of any State may empower the executive thereof to make temporary appointments until the people fill the vacancies by election as the legislature may direct.

This amendment shall not be so construed as to affect the election or term of any Senator chosen before it becomes valid as part of the Constitution. (Ratified April, 1913.)

## AMENDMENT XVIII

### Section 1

After one year from the ratification of this article the manufacture, sale, or transportation of intoxicating liquors within, the importation thereof into, or the exportation thereof from the United States and all territory subject to the jurisdiction thereof for beverage purposes is hereby prohibited.

### Section 2

The Congress and the several States shall have concurrent power to enforce this article by appropriate legislation.

## Section 3

This article shall be inoperative unless it shall have been ratified as an amendment to the Constitution by the legislatures of the several States, as provided in the Constitution, within seven years from the date of the submission hereof to the States by the Congress.][2] (Ratified January, 1919.)

## AMENDMENT XIX

The right of citizens of the United States to vote shall not be denied or abridged by the United States or by any State on account of sex.

Congress shall have power to enforce this article by appropriate legislation. (Ratified August, 1920.)

## AMENDMENT XX

### Section 1

The terms of the President and Vice President shall end at noon on the 20th day of January, and the terms of Senators and Representatives at noon on the 3d day of January, of the years in which such terms would have ended if this article had not been ratified; and the terms of their successors shall then begin.

### Section 2

The Congress shall assemble at least once in every year, and such meeting shall begin at noon on the 3d day of January, unless they shall by law appoint a different day.

### Section 3

If, at the time fixed for the beginning of the term of the President, the President elect shall have died, the Vice President elect shall become President. If a President shall not have been chosen before the time fixed for the beginning of his term, or if the President elect shall have failed to qualify, then the Vice President elect shall act as President until a President shall have qualified; and the Congress may by law provide for the case wherein neither a President elect nor a Vice President elect shall have qualified, declaring who shall then act as President, or the manner in which one who is to act shall be selected, and such person shall act accordingly until a President or Vice President shall have qualified.

### Section 4

The Congress may by law provide for the case of the death of any of the persons from whom the House of Representatives may choose a President whenever the right of choice shall have devolved upon them, and for the case of the death of any of the persons from whom the Senate may choose a Vice President whenever the right of choice shall have devolved upon them.

### Section 5

Sections I and 2 shall take effect on the 15th day of October following the ratification of this article.

---

[2] Repealed by the Twenty-first Amendment.

## Section 6

This article shall be inoperative unless it shall have been ratified as an amendment to the Constitution by the legislatures of three-fourths of the several States within seven years from the date of its submission. (Ratified January, 1933.)

## AMENDMENT XXI

### Section 1

The eighteenth article of amendment to the Constitution of the United States is hereby repealed.

### Section 2

The transportation or importation into any State, Territory, or possession of the United States for delivery or use therein of intoxicating liquors, in violation of the laws thereof, is hereby prohibited.

### Section 3

This article shall be inoperative unless it shall have been ratified as an amendment to the Constitution by conventions in the several States, as provided in the Constitution, within seven years from the date of the submission hereof to the States by the Congress. (Ratified December, 1933.)

## AMENDMENT XXII

### Section I

No person shall be elected to the office of the President more than twice, and no person who has held the office of President, or acted as President, for more than two years of a term to which some other person was elected President shall be elected to the office of the President more than once. But this Article shall not apply to any person holding the office of President when this Article was proposed by the Congress, and shall not prevent any person who may be holding the office of President, or acting as President, during the term within which this Article becomes operative from holding the office of President or acting as President during the remainder of such term.

### Section 2

This article shall be inoperative unless it shall have been ratified as an amendment to the Constitution by the legislatures of three-fourths of the several States within seven years from the date of its submission to the States by the Congress. (Ratified February, 1951.)

## AMENDMENT XXIII

### Section 1

The District constituting the seat of Government of the United States shall appoint in such manner as the Congress may direct:

A number of electors of President and Vice President equal to the whole number of Senators and Representatives in Congress to which the District would be entitled if it were a State, but in no event more than the least populous State; they shall be in addition to those appointed by the States, but they shall be considered, for the purposes of the election of President and Vice President, to be electors appointed by a State; and they shall meet in the District and perform such duties as provided by the twelfth article of amendment.

## Section 2

The Congress shall have power to enforce this article by appropriate legislation. (Ratified March, 1961.)

## AMENDMENT XXIV

### Section 1

The right of citizens of the United States to vote in any primary or other election for President or Vice President, for electors for President or Vice President, or for Senator or Representative in Congress, shall not be denied or abridged by the United States or any State by reason of failure to pay any poll tax or other tax.

### Section 2

The Congress shall have power to enforce this article by appropriate legislation. (Ratified January, 1964.)

## AMENDMENT XXV

### Section 1

In case of the removal of the President from office or of his death or resignation, the Vice President shall become President.

### Section 2

Whenever there is a vacancy in the office of the Vice President, the President shall nominate a Vice President who shall take office upon confirmation by a majority vote of both Houses of Congress.

### Section 3

Whenever the President transmits to the President pro tempore of the Senate and the Speaker of the House of Representatives his written declaration that he is unable to discharge the powers and duties of his office, and until he transmits to them a written declaration to the contrary, such powers and duties shall be discharged by the Vice President as Acting President.

### Section 4

Whenever the Vice President and a majority of either the principal officers of the executive departments or of such other body as Congress may by law provide, transmit to the President pro tempore of the Senate and the Speaker of the House of Representatives their written declaration that the President is unable to discharge the powers and duties of his office, the Vice President shall immediately assume the powers and duties of the office as Acting President.

Thereafter, when the President transmits to the President pro tempore of the Senate and the Speaker of the House of Representatives his written declaration that no inability exists, he shall resume the powers and duties of his office unless the Vice President and a majority of either the principal officers of the executive department or of such other body as Congress may by law provide, transmit within four days to the President pro tempore of the Senate and the Speaker of the House of Representatives their written declaration that the President is unable to discharge the powers and duties of his office. Thereupon Congress shall decide the issue, assembling within forty-eight hours for that purpose if not in session. If the Congress, within twenty-one days after receipt of the latter written declaration, or, if Congress is not in session, within twenty-one days after

Congress is required to assemble, determines by two-thirds vote of both Houses that the President is unable to discharge the powers and duties of his office, the Vice President shall continue to discharge the same as Acting President; otherwise, the President shall resume the powers and duties of his office. (Ratified February, 1967.)

## AMENDMENT XXVI

### Section I

The right of citizens of the United States, who are eighteen years of age or older, to vote shall not be denied or abridged by the United States or by any State on account of age.

### Section 2

The Congress shall have power to enforce this article by appropriate legislation. (Ratified July, 1971.)

## AMENDMENT XXVII

No law varying the compensation for the services of the Senators or Representatives, shall take effect, until an election of Representatives shall have intervened. (Ratified May, 1992.)

# Answers for Exercises

## 1 Domino Effect

### Remember the Story (pp. 4 and 5)

1. Eddie Buchanan to Jenny Tang
2. Mayor Reilly to Eddie Buchanan
3. Tom Furlong to Eddie Buchanan
4. Carla Castillo to TV audience
5. Vince Polito to Tom Furlong
6. Marsha Buchanan to Tom Furlong

a. 5   b. 1   c. 6   d. 4   e. 3   f. 2

1. hostage
2. citation
3. city hall
4. negotiate
5. paramedic
6. evacuate

Answers may vary. Here are some possible answers.

1. Yes, I saw Eddie Buchanan take the gun away from the guard.
2. He was angry because the city put a boot on his car.
3. They came into the room through the ceiling and captured Buchanan without anyone else getting hurt.
4. They should hire more security guards.

### Remember Turning Points (pp. 6 and 7)

1. T   2. T   3. F   4. T   5. F

a. 6   b. 2   c. 3   d. 1   e. 5   f. 4

1. **Group:** British government
   **Action:** taxed colonists
   **Result of Action:** colonists became angry about taxation without representation

2. **Group:** First Continental Congress
   **Action:** agreed to cut trade off with Britain, agreed to meet the following year if the situation did not improve
   **Result of Action:** situation got worse; fighting began in Massachusetts

3. **Group:** Second Continental Congress
   **Action:** debated whether to form a government that was independent of Great Britain
   **Result of Action:** the Declaration of Independence

### Making Connections (p. 7)

1. Eddie Buchanan (1 point)
2. Mayor Reilly (1 point)

1. a. The government tried to negotiate with Buchanan. During the rescue of the hostages, Buchanan was shot and later arrested. (1 point)
   b. The government tried to rescue the hostages. (1 point)
   c. The government tried to rescue Venderbrook. (1 point)
   d. The government warned other citizens of the situation and evacuated them from the area. (1 point)

1. Some people are injured, all are rescued, and Buchanan is arrested. (3 points)
2. If the government had not tried to rescue the hostages, Buchanan might have shot more people. (1 point)

## Find Out More: Key Ideas (p. 10)

1. **a.** In a society, government consists of the people and institutions with authority to make, carry out, and enforce laws.
2. **a.** Government provides the services that cannot be accomplished without a collective effort—national, state, or local.
3. **a.** Totalitarian governments go a step further. They attempt to control every aspect of the lives of individuals and forbid people to freely associate with one another to accomplish their goals.
4. **b.** Authority is power combined with the right to use that power.

Answers may vary. Here are some possible answers.

1. to maintain law and order, protect national security, provide public services, and uphold democracy.
2. we would have no good way to settle arguments or protect people from crime.   OR
   we would have no good way to defend ourselves from attacks.   OR
   we would not have major roads or highways.

Answers may vary. Here are some possible answers.

1. Yes. Government protects individual rights and the common good. It provides organization and maintains law and order. Government defends the country during war and protects people from crime. Government provides services that people need. Government provides a way for people to do things together that they cannot do alone.
2. Answers are based on personal opinion.

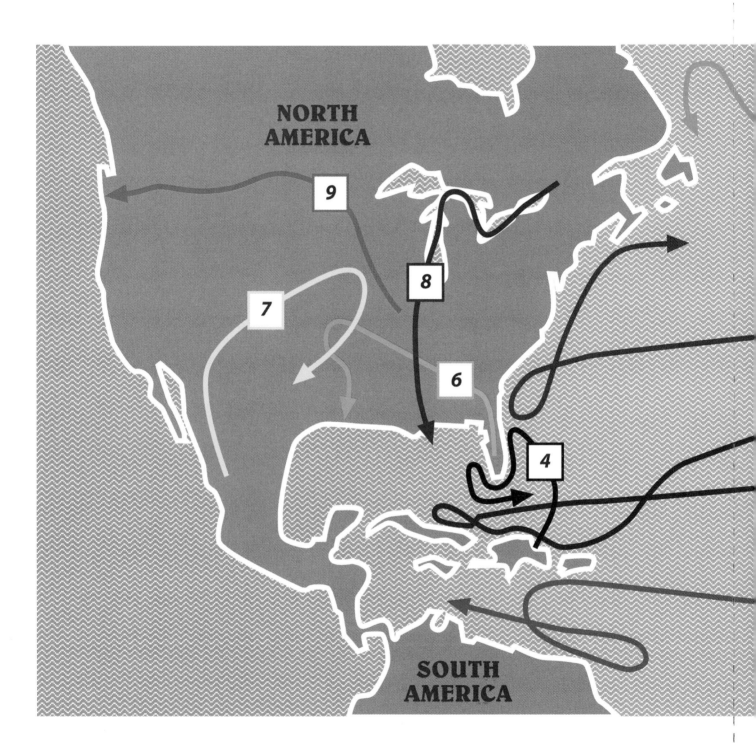

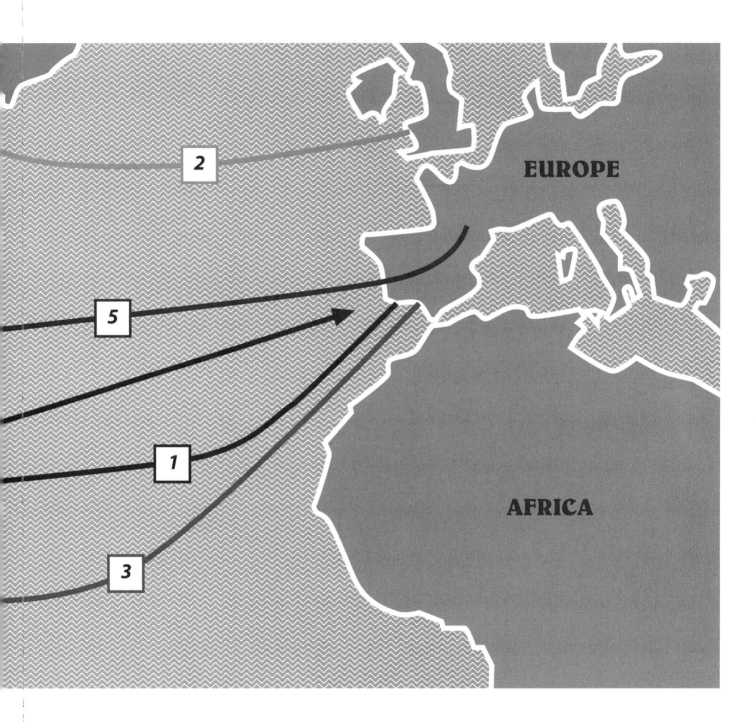

# Answers for Exercises

## 2   Like Taking Candy From a Baby

### Remember the Story  (pp. 18 and 19)

1. Carla Castillo to Mr. Tang
2. Mr. Tang to Carla Castillo and Jenny Tang
3. Marty Siegel to Diane Clayton and Derek Powell
4. Mark Taglioni to Marty Siegel, Derek Powell, and Diane Clayton
5. Vince to Mark Taglioni
6. Jenny Tang to Mr. Tang

a.  4      b.  5      c.  3      d.  2      e.  1

| 1. mortgage | 3. illegal | 5. scam | 7. documented |
|---|---|---|---|
| 2. contract | 4. fraud | 6. under duress | |

Answers may vary.  Here are some possible answers.

1. Because we needed evidence that Vince was breaking the law.
2. We wanted to have enough evidence to convince a jury that he is guilty.   OR
   We wanted to eliminate reasonable doubt.
3. I hope that a jury will convict him and he will go to prison.   OR
   He will go to trial.
4. Make sure he understands any contract before he signs it.

### Remember Turning Points  (pp. 20 and 21)

1. T      2. T      3. F      4. F      5. T

a.  1787      b.  1776      c.  1776      d.  1787      e.  1776      f.  1787

CONTINENTAL CONGRESS AND ARTICLES OF CONFEDERATION (1776)

**c.** Congress has no money or power.
**e.** States form a weak coalition.
**b.** Congress has no authority to settle disputes.

CONSTITUTIONAL CONVENTION (1787)

**f.** Delegates agree on a strong government.
**d.** Delegates compromise on representation in Congress.
**a.** Authority is shared and controlled.

### After the Constitutional Convention

1. a strong national government
2. a two-house legislature
3. a president
4. a court system

## Making Connections (p. 21)

Mitch, Vince, and others who are involved in the scam. (1 point)

All three. (1 point)
- The police collect the evidence against Vince and Mitch. (1 point)
- The district attorney, an elected official, decides whether or not the evidence is enough for a jury to convict. (1 point)
- The Tangs, ordinary citizens, cooperate with the police in order to get evidence. (1 point)

Both. (1 point)
- The district attorney's office and the police help Mr. Tang, the victim, by secretly videotaping Mitch threatening Mr. Tang. When Mr. Tang is threatened with violence, the police come to his rescue. (1 point)
- The district attorney will not charge Vince or Mitch with a crime without clear evidence. Taglioni's tape of telephone conversations only records one side of the conversations, so there is no evidence of a victim. The jury would probably not convict Vince or Mitch with only the tape as evidence. (1 point)

## Find Out More: Key Ideas (p. 24)

1. **c.** No one is above the law.
2. **a.** The basis for the rule of law in the United States is the Constitution.
3. **b.** The Preamble, or introduction, states that the purpose of government in the United States is to . . . insure domestic tranquility.
4. **c.** Executive power was given to the position of president rather than to a committee of leaders.

Answers may vary. Here are some possible answers.

1. to tell people how to behave; to protect rights; to give people benefits; to give people responsibilities; and to prevent people in authority from having too much power
2. the legislative, executive, and judicial branches

Answers may vary. Here are some possible answers.

1. Laws make rules for behavior. If people do not follow these rules, they may be punished. For example, laws prohibit stealing and murder. Drivers must follow traffic laws.
2. Some of the responsibilities we have under the Constitution are to obey the law, to vote, and to pay taxes. Some of the benefits are defense against an invasion from another country, the freedom to practice different religions, and personal freedoms for ourselves and our children.

**Inside Information** (p. 26)

| Conflict | Years | Major Opponents | Results |
|---|---|---|---|
| The War of 1812 | 1812–1814 | United States vs. Great Britain | The United States remained independent. |
| The Mexican War | 1846–1848 | United States vs. Mexico | *Rio Grande becomes the border between U. S. and Mexico. New Mexico and California added to the United States.* |
| The U.S. Civil War | 1861–1865 | *Northern vs. Southern States* | Union of states preserved. Slavery ended. |
| The Spanish-American War | *1898* | United States vs. Spain | United States gained control of Puerto Rico, Guam, Philippines. |
| World War I | 1914–1918 | Allies (France, Britain, Russia, Japan, and later Italy [1915] and the United States [1917]) vs. Central Powers (Germany, Austria-Hungary, Turkey, Bulgaria) | *Central Powers defeated. The Austro-Hungarian Empire dismantled with new states established in Eastern Europe. Germany disarmed, stripped of her colonial empire in addition to loss of land in Europe, and forced to pay huge reparations.* |
| World War II | 1939–1945 | *Allies (France, Britain, China, and later the Soviet Union [1940] and the United States [1941], along with many other nations of the world) vs. Axis (Germany, Italy, Japan)* | Axis powers defeated. Territory and weapons taken from them. Money demanded for damages inflicted. Military leaders tried and punished. |
| The Korean Conflict | 1950–1953 | South Korea, supported by United Nations troops (including United States) vs. North Korea, supported by People's Republic of China | *Korea continues to be divided into two separate countries.* |
| The Vietnam Conflict | 1961–1975 | *South Vietnam supported by U.S. troops and others vs. North Vietnam and Viet Cong guerillas* | Government of South Vietnam resigned. Country unified under North Vietnamese control. United States withdraws all troops. |

# Answers for Exercises

## 3   For the Greater Good

### Remember the Story  (pp. 30 and 31)

🔔
1. Bill Garrison to City Council
2. Juan Castillo to City Council
3. Ernesto to Juan Castillo
4. Mike Rodriguez to David Malone and Bill Garrison
5. Carla Castillo to David Malone

🔔🔔
a. 1     b. 4     c. 2     d. 5     e. 3

1. resolution        4. campaign
2. mayor             5. compromise
3. city council      6. district

🔔🔔🔔
Answers may vary.  Here are some possible answers.

1. You must be sad to leave this house.
2. They think the project will help our community.
3. He thinks the highway will give young people more opportunities.
4. We will lose some of the places we love, but our community will not be destroyed.

### Remember Turning Points  (pp. 32 and 33)

🔔
1. F        2. F        3. T        4. T        5. F

🔔🔔
1. b        2. d        3. g        4. c        5. a        6. f        7. e

🔔🔔🔔

| People and Groups | Role in Developing the Bill of Rights |
|---|---|
| 1. Opponents of the Constitution | pushed for amendments that specified personal rights |
| 2. Supporters of the Constitution | agreed to add a bill of rights to the Constitution |
| 3. U.S. Representative James Madison | reviewed changes to the Constitution suggested by the state conventions; recommended a group of amendments to Congress |
| 4. U.S. Congress | debated, revised, and approved the amendments |
| 5. The states | ratified the amendments |

## Making Connections (p. 33)

1. Juan Castillo and some people in his community think their homes and businesses are being threatened. (1 point)
2. Mike Hernandez represents Moreno Heights on the City Council. (1 point)
3. Juan Castillo leads them in their fight to protect the Moreno Heights neighborhood. (1 point)

1. The Madison Highway Extension Project is threatening their rights. (1 point)
2. Even though they will receive money for their property, residents will be forced to move. (1 point)
3. a. Juan Castillo, the leader of the people in the community, was not happy about the project; he organized people in his community to oppose it. (1 point)
   b. At first, Mike Hernandez, the people's representative on the City Council, seemed to support the people who opposed the project. But in the end he voted for the project. (1 point)
   c. Carla recognizes that the highway extension will be good for the city and many of the people who live in Moreno Heights. But for older residents, the move will be very painful. (1 point)

1. The project ends up being approved by the City Council. (1 point)
   Mike Hernandez votes in favor of it. (1 point)
2. The project could have been defeated by the City Council. (1 point)

## Find Out More: Key Ideas (p. 36)

1. **a.** The supporters of the Constitution were called Federalists.
2. **b.** In spring 1790, the last of the thirteen states, Rhode Island, approved the Constitution.
3. **a.** They called these amendments the "Bill of Rights."
4. **c.** Amendment 1: Freedom of Religion and Expression: Congress cannot establish an official religion or interfere with freedom of worship.

Answers may vary. Here are some possible answers.

1. many people did not support it.   OR
   delegates at the state conventions debated for many months.
2. • protect individual rights
   • limit the power of the central government
   • convince the Anti-Federalists to ratify the Constitution

Answers may vary. Here are some possible answers.

1. The Anti-Federalists thought that the Constitution gave too much power to the central government. They thought that the Constitution did not protect individual rights.
2. Answers will come from personal experience.

## Inside Information (p. 38)

1. The colors are red, white, and blue.
2. The stripes represent each of the original thirteen colonies.
3. There is a star for each state.
4. Alaska and Hawaii were the last two states to become part of the United States.

## 4  Between a Rock and a Hard Place

### Remember the Story  (pp. 42 and 43)

1. Councilman Prescott to James Wagner
2. James Wagner to Councilman Prescott
3. Derek Powell to Jess Holcomb
4. Jess Holcomb to Derek Powell
5. James Wagner to Mitchell Wagner
6. Mitchell Wagner to James Wagner

a. 2    b. 5    c. 4    d. 3    e. 1

1. motion
2. ruling
3. obstruction of public property
4. federal guideline
5. appeal
6. comply
7. disabled
8. coalition

Answers may vary.  Here are some possible answers.

1. His father believes in the legal process.  James broke the law to make his point.
2. It convinced me of the dangers of buildings that are difficult to enter or leave.
3. We have to find the money somehow.
4. We have to balance the interests of all groups.

### Remember Turning Points  (pp. 44 and 45)

1. a    2. b    3. c    4. a    5. c    6. b

1. Federalism
2. Separation of powers
3. Checks and balances

Answers may vary.  Here are some possible answers.

1. • Congress
   • FUNCTION: makes laws; approves or rejects presidential appointments; declares war
   • LIMITS: The president can approve or veto the laws.

2. • the president
   • FUNCTION: carries out the laws; sets national goals; develops policies
   • LIMITS: The Senate must approve his appointments.

3. • the courts
   • FUNCTION: resolves disputes involving the laws; determines whether laws passed by Congress and actions of the president are constitutional
   • LIMITS: Federal judges are appointed by the president and approved by the Senate.

## Making Connections (p. 45)

1. a law that says that buildings must be safe and accessible for disabled people (1 point)
2. Congress passed the law, the president signed it. (1 point)
3. a lack of funds (1 point)

1. • James's approach is to take action. (1 point)
   • Mitchell's approach is to work with the system, to talk to people, and to convince them that the changes are necessary. He knows that changes will not occur quickly, but he is willing to work with government officials. (1 point)
2. The father thinks that they are making progress. The son feels that things aren't changing quickly enough. (1 point)

1. by ruling that the law must be enforced (1 point)

2. • Congress could vote to change the law. Congress could provide funding to cities to make buildings more accessible to the disabled. (1 point)
   • Representatives from the Department of Justice could pressure the city to enforce the law. (1 point)
   • The court could rule that the law is unfair so the city doesn't have to comply. (1 point)

## Find Out More: Key Ideas (p. 48)

1. **a.** Federalism is a system that divides power between the states and the national government.
2. **c.** For example, both levels of government have the power to tax the people.
3. **b.** Bills passed by both houses of Congress become law with president's signature.
4. **c.** The Senate has the power to accept or reject these nominations.

Answers may vary. Here are some possible answers.

1. the control of trade between states and with other nations.   OR
   the declaration of war.   OR
   the printing and issuing of money.
2. voters elect members of Congress to a term of office.   OR
   the president can veto a bill.   OR
   the Supreme Court can declare a law unconstitutional.

Answers may vary. Here are some possible answers.

1. Congress writes, debates, and votes on bills. The President signs bills to make them laws. The Supreme Court interprets laws. The Supreme Court can decide that a law is unfair.
2. Advantages: No one branch of government can gain too much power.
   Disadvantages: It could take longer to get things done.

## Inside Information (p. 50)

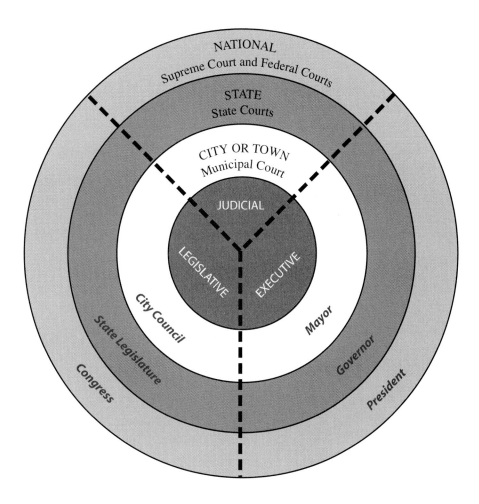

## 5  Collision Course, Part 1

### Remember the Matthews Family's Story  (pp. 56 and 57)

1. Paul Tremaine to workers
2. Linda Matthews to Ray Matthews
3. Linda Matthews to Jenny Tang and Diane Clayton
4. Ray Matthews to Linda Matthews
5. Linda Matthews to Ray Matthews

a.  4     b.  1     c.  5     d.  2     e.  3

1. competitive
2. contract
3. benefits
4. minimum wage
5. temp agency
6. profit
7. welfare

Answers may vary.  Here are some possible answers.

1. You don't understand.  Sanford is just telling the truth.
2. Foreigners are destroying our country.
3. I can't find a job because the government lets factories move to other countries where people work for almost nothing.
4. Times have changed.  No one wants to hire a good machinist unless he has other skills.

### Remember Clay Sanford's Story  (pp. 54 and 55)

1. Clay Sanford to crowd
2. Carla Castillo to TV audience
3. Dave Kinnard to Carla Castillo
4. Clay Sanford to Francisco and Hector Lopez
5. Hector Lopez to Clay Sanford

a.  3     b.  5     c.  2     d.  1     e.  4

1. permit
2. riot
3. free speech
4. suspend
5. discriminates
6. scapegoats

Answers may vary.  Here are some possible answers.

1. Good.  Notify all the news media.
2. I don't think it will be necessary, but be ready just in case.
3. I threatened to tell the news media that they discriminated against me.
4. They will be very careful not to interfere with my right to free speech.

### Remember Turning Points  (pp. 58 and 59)

1.  e     2.  c     3.  a     4.  b     5.  d     6.  b     7.  b and f

1. Europeans
2. Africans
3. Spaniards
4. Mexicans
5. Chinese
6. Southeast Asians

Answers may vary.  Here are some possible answers.

1. Europeans in the 1600s
2. Latin Americans today and Southeast Asians in the 1970s and 1980s
3. Europeans in the 1600s, Chinese in the 1800s, Asians and Latin Americans today

## Making Connections (p. 59)

1. Clay Sanford's message  (1 point)
2. This message appeals to unemployed workers.  (1 point)
3. immigrants from Ray Matthews and other unemployed workers  (2 points)

1. The message is that immigrants have put millions of "real" Americans out of work.  (1 point)
2. Supporters and opponents begin to fight, so the police stop the rally.  (1 point)

1. Sanford decides to file a lawsuit against the city.  (1 point)
   He feels his freedom of speech was violated.  (1 point)
2. He gets Francisco and Hector Lopez to represent him.  (1 point)
3. The Lopezes could have chosen not to represent him, but then they might have been accused of discrimination.  (1 point)

## Find Out More: Key Ideas  (p. 62)

1. **b.** Many personal freedoms guaranteed by the Constitution are found in the First Amendment.
2. **a.** But all the settlers wanted was the chance to own their own land.
3. **a.** The degree of religious tolerance they found in the new country was unusual for its time.
4. **b.** Today laws limit the number of people who can immigrate to the United States each year.

Answers may vary.  Here are some possible answers.

1. Congress cannot pass laws to restrict freedom of expression.
2. The United States is one country populated by millions of immigrants from many different nations.

Answers may vary.  Here are some possible answers.

1. Many European countries had a single established religion.  People who believed differently were persecuted.  In the different colonies, many different religions were practiced.
2. Immigration policies have allowed many people with different cultures and languages to come together to create the United States.

## Inside Information  (p. 64)

1. White House
2. Capitol
3. Bald Eagle
4. Liberty Bell
5. Statue of Liberty
6. The Great Seal

A. 4
B. 6
C. 5

_3_

_4_

_5_

_1_

_2_

_6_

## 6 Collision Course, Part 2

### Remember the Story (pp. 68 and 69)

1. Hector Lopez to Francisco Lopez
2. Francisco Lopez to Hector Lopez
3. Mayor Reilly to Jess Holcomb
4. Hector Lopez to Francisco Lopez
5. Linda Matthews to Ray Matthews
6. Clay Sanford to Hector Lopez
7. Carla Castillo to TV audience

a. 3     b. 1     c. 5     d. 6     e. 4     f. 2

1. violated          3. bigot          5. continuance
2. biased            4. traitor        6. controversial

Answers may vary. Here are some possible answers.

1. When he has fully recovered.
2. I'm glad the court upheld the Constitution.
3. I think the city clearly violated your right to free speech.
4. I don't want to hear your speeches. Your message offends me.

### Remember Turning Points (pp. 70 and 71)

1. a     2. a     3. a     4. a     5. a     6. a

1. Jewish survivors of Nazi concentration camps settle in Skokie
2. Nazis apply for parade permit
3. City passes laws to stop parade
4. American Nazi Party takes case to court
5. First Amendment for everyone
6. First Amendment not for people who want to destroy freedom
7. Supreme Court rules in favor of Nazi Party

Answers may vary. Here are some possible answers.

**Reasons to Restrict**

• People who encourage hate may create unnecessary problems between groups of people.
• People who speak out and urge public protests against the government may be the cause of riots and other disturbances.
• Children won't know what to believe if they hear people speaking against their country and its government.
• People who receive government services shouldn't criticize the government.

**Reasons Not to Restrict**

- If people have the freedom to say what they think, they can influence other people and achieve change over time.
- New discoveries can be made if people talk to one another and share information.
- Freedom of speech has meaning only if we give people we disagree with the opportunity to speak as well.
- People can make better decisions when they have all the information they need, not just part of it.

## Making Connections (p. 71)

1. Clay Sanford (1 point)
2. Francisco Lopez (1 point)
3. Francisco's son, Hector Lopez (1 point)

1. Francisco Lopez is attacked by someone and hospitalized. (1 point)
2. The decision is that the city is guilty of violating Sanford's First Amendment right to free speech. (1 point)

1. The father and son disagree because the father recognizes that free speech is for everyone, even people he disagrees with. But the son has trouble separating the right to free speech from what a person says. (2 points)
2. The son changes his opinion when he sees his father attacked for his ideas. (1 point)
3. Answers may vary. Here are some possible answers. (1 point)
   - If the father hadn't been attacked, the son might not have changed his opinion.
   - If the city had allowed the rally to continue, people might have been hurt. They could have sued the city for not stopping the rally.
   - Sanford might have lost the case, and then he and the Lopez firm would have appealed.

## Find Out More: Key Ideas (p. 74)

1. **a.** Thus, the only way to protect freedom of speech was to protect it for all people, no matter how disagreeable their ideas might be.
2. **c.** Freedom of speech does not guarantee "good information," but it does increase the chances of people getting it.
3. **a.** The federal government and thirty three states also passed laws making it illegal to promote rebellion against the United States.
4. **c.** When freedom of expression is dangerous to public safety or national security, the courts have sometimes allowed freedom of expression to be limited.

Answers may vary. Here are some possible answers.

1. in the colonies, some people had died for saying what they believed.   OR
   they did not think that the government should decide which beliefs are acceptable.
2. people can express their ideas openly and try to convince others to make peaceful changes.

1. Answers may vary. Here are some possible answers.

   • After President McKinley was killed, many states made it a crime to promote the overthrow of the government.   OR
   • After World War I, the government prosecuted people for supporting draft resistance, mass strikes, or the overthrow of government.   OR
   • In 1949, eleven communist leaders were convicted of working for the violent overthrow of the government.

2. Answers will depend on personal experience.

## Inside Information (p. 76)

1.          laws

2.          Congress

3 and 4     Senate, House of Representatives

5 and 6     Each state has two senators. The number of people in the House of Representatives depends on the population of the state.

7, 8, and 9  Answers may vary. Here are some possible answers.
   • the power to tax
   • the power to create a court system
   • the power to declare war
   • the power to coin money and regulate its value
   • the power to regulate commerce with foreign nations and among the states
   • the power to establish rules related to naturalization

   Three correct answers are all that you need!

10.         A bill is a proposed law that is sent to both houses of Congress for approval.

11.         A law is a bill that has been approved by both houses of Congress and signed by the president.

12.         step 1: A member of Congress has an idea for a new law. He or she writes down the idea and proposes it to other members of Congress. This written idea is called a bill.

13.         step 2: The bill is approved by the House of Representatives.

14.         step 3: The bill is approved by the Senate.

15.         step 4: If the president approves the bill and signs it, it becomes a law. If the president vetoes the bill, then it can become a law only if two-thirds of the members of Congress vote for it.

16.         The Supreme Court has the power to declare unconstitutional a law made by Congress. If that happens, the law cannot be enforced.

17.         The president can veto a bill.

## 7 A Delicate Balance

### Remember the Story (pp. 80 and 81)

🔔 1. Warren Talbot to reporters
2. Assistant District Attorney Marty Siegel to Prosecuting Attorneys
3. Prosecuting attorneys to Carla Castillo
4. Carla Castillo to Steve Richardson, News Producer
5. Warren Talbot to Susan Miller
6. Susan Miller to Carla Castillo

🔔🔔 a. 6     b. 3     c. 1     d. 4     e. 2     f. 5

1. anonymous          3. contempt of court        5. hearsay
2. source             4. subpoena                 6. out-of-court settlement

🔔🔔🔔 Answers may vary. Here are some possible answers.

1. For not revealing my source for the Talbot case.
2. I promised not to tell anyone her name.
3. Sometimes my sources ask to be anonymous. But as a reporter I must verify every story before I report it to the public.
4. No, I have a right to protect my sources of information.   OR
   Yes, the judge is following the law.

### Remember Turning Points (pp. 82 and 83)

🔔 1. T     2. T     3. F     4. T     5. F

🔔🔔 
Totalitarian Government     1     3     5
Democracy                   2     4     6

🔔🔔🔔 Answers may vary. Here are some possible answers.

1. People in a community have the right to know what their city council is doing.
2. Reporters must check the facts before they print a story.
3. In wartime, reporters cannot give information that would place the country or its military in danger.
4. Reporters who print information they know to be untrue can be sued.

### Making Connections (p. 83)

🔔 1. Carla Castillo and *Metro 5 News* represent the press.
2. Carla is asked to name her source.

🔔🔔 1. The attorneys in the assistant district attorney's office wanted Carla to reveal her source. They said the woman's testimony could help convict Talbot. They believed the state's case was weak without her testimony.

1. The news producer at *Metro 5 News* agreed to let Carla report information from an anonymous source. Carla refused to reveal her source of information. As a result, the judge said she was in contempt of court and sent her to jail. (1 point)

2. • The station could have refused to let Carla report the information from her source because it was anonymous.    OR
   • Carla could have revealed her source, but then no one would want to give her information in the future. (1 point)

## Find Out More: Key Ideas (p. 86)

1. **b.** As a result, the English governor outlawed all printing presses in the colony.
2. **a.** After a long trial, the jury decided that Zenger had published the truth about the governor.
3. **c.** The press has the right to report about government actions and the work of government officials.
4. **b.** When the nation is at war, government may try to control the release of information that could endanger the U.S. military or the country in general.

Answers may vary. Here are some possible answers.

1. they gave people information about the government and encouraged people to criticize the government.
2. the jury's decision encouraged other colonists to work for freedom of the press.

Answers may vary. Here are some possible answers.

1. The press is free to investigate government and tell people what government is doing. Then people can express opinions about the government's activities. When people do not agree with government, they can tell their elected representatives, or they can protest.
2. Answers will come from learner's personal experience.

The crossword puzzle solution:

Across:
1. LAW S
3. CABINET
6. SIGN
7. STATE
11. CHIEF
12. UNION
14. VETO
15. TWO

Down:
2. SENATE (SENAR...)
3. COURT
4. BILL
5. TREATY
8. EXECUTIVE
9. APPOINT
10. WRIT
13. FOUR
14. VICE

# Score Sheet for Answers for Exercises

After you check your answers, use the score sheet to record the number correct. Your teacher or tutor may want to see your scores.

## Unit 1, Domino Effect

| | 🔔 | 🔔🔔 | 🔔🔔🔔 |
|---|---|---|---|
| Remember the Story | ___ out of 6 | ___ out of 12 | ___ out of 4 |
| Remember Turning Points | ___ out of 5 | ___ out of 6 | ___ out of 6 |
| Making Connections | ___ out of 2 | ___ out of 4 | ___ out of 3 |
| Find Out More: Key Ideas | ___ out of 8 | ___ out of 2 | ___ out of 2 |

## Unit 2, Like Taking Candy from a Baby

| | 🔔 | 🔔🔔 | 🔔🔔🔔 |
|---|---|---|---|
| Remember the Story | ___ out of 6 | ___ out of 12 | ___ out of 4 |
| Remember Turning Points | ___ out of 5 | ___ out of 6 | ___ out of 4 |
| Making Connections | ___ out of 1 | ___ out of 4 | ___ out of 3 |
| Find Out More: Key Ideas | ___ out of 8 | ___ out of 2 | ___ out of 2 |

## Unit 3, For the Greater Good

| | 🔔 | 🔔🔔 | 🔔🔔🔔 |
|---|---|---|---|
| Remember the Story | ___ out of 5 | ___ out of 11 | ___ out of 4 |
| Remember Turning Points | ___ out of 5 | ___ out of 7 | ___ out of 5 |
| Making Connections | ___ out of 3 | ___ out of 5 | ___ out of 3 |
| Find Out More: Key Ideas | ___ out of 8 | ___ out of 2 | ___ out of 2 |

## Unit 4, Between a Rock and a Hard Place

| | 🔔 | 🔔🔔 | 🔔🔔🔔 |
|---|---|---|---|
| Remember the Story | ___ out of 6 | ___ out of 13 | ___ out of 4 |
| Remember Turning Points | ___ out of 6 | ___ out of 3 | ___ out of 12 |
| Making Connections | ___ out of 3 | ___ out of 3 | ___ out of 4 |
| Find Out More: Key Ideas | ___ out of 8 | ___ out of 2 | ___ out of 2 |

## Unit 5, Collision Course, Part 1

| | 🔔 | 🔔 🔔 | 🔔 🔔 🔔 |
|---|---|---|---|
| Remember the Matthews Family's Story | ___ out of 5 | ___ out of 12 | ___ out of 4 |
| Remember Clay Sanford's Story | ___ out of 5 | ___ out of 11 | ___ out of 4 |
| Remember Turning Points | ___ out of 7 | ___ out of 6 | ___ out of 3 |
| Making Connections | ___ out of 4 | ___ out of 2 | ___ out of 4 |
| Find Out More: Key Ideas | ___ out of 8 | ___ out of 2 | ___ out of 2 |

## Unit 6, Collision Course, Part 2

| | 🔔 | 🔔 🔔 | 🔔 🔔 🔔 |
|---|---|---|---|
| Remember the Story | ___ out of 7 | ___ out of 12 | ___ out of 4 |
| Remember Turning Points | ___ out of 6 | ___ out of 7 | ___ out of 6 |
| Making Connections | ___ out of 3 | ___ out of 2 | ___ out of 4 |
| Find Out More: Key Ideas | ___ out of 8 | ___ out of 2 | ___ out of 2 |

## Unit 7, A Delicate Balance

| | 🔔 | 🔔 🔔 | 🔔 🔔 🔔 |
|---|---|---|---|
| Remember the Story | ___ out of 6 | ___ out of 12 | ___ out of 4 |
| Remember Turning Points | ___ out of 5 | ___ out of 6 | ___ out of 4 |
| Making Connections | ___ out of 2 | ___ out of 1 | ___ out of 2 |
| Find Out More: Key Ideas | ___ out of 8 | ___ out of 2 | ___ out of 2 |

# 1 Check Your Progress on *Domino Effect*

### ⚖ Check Your Memory

**Answer the questions.**

1. What is government?

2. What types of services can a government provide?

3. What are the purposes of government in the United States?

4. What events led to the establishment of a new government by the colonists?

5. What positive things can happen when people work together?

6. What is the difference between authority and power?

*To check your answers, look on pages 144 and 145. Record your score here.* ☐

*If your score is 4 or more points, go to* ⚖⚖.

### ⚖ ⚖ Make It Real

**Read the situations and answer the questions.**

1. What can the government do to promote the common good in each situation?

   a. Grantstown had a flood. The river overflowed and flooded the streets and buildings. Some people were surrounded by water. The water cut off the electricity and contaminated the drinking water.

   b. Millett County is far from any town. Farmers there grow vegetables. They want to sell their crops, but the roads are not paved. Trucks cannot travel to Millett County to transport the crops.

   c. A group says they will put a bomb on a passenger airplane somewhere in the United States.

2. The colonists who started the American Revolution said, "No taxation without representation!" Read the story. Is this a situation of taxation without representation? Why or why not?

   The people of Jonesville elected Mayor Hanson and the city council members. After the election, the mayor and the City Council decided to increase the city tax on cars. Many people protested, but the city still increased the tax. In the next election, people elected Mike Jahn as the new mayor.

*To check your answers, look on page 145. Record your score here.* ☐

*If your score is 4 or more points, go to* ⚖⚖⚖.

You Be the Judge

**Read the story. Then answer the questions.**

Sarah owns her house. She received a property tax bill in the mail. The tax is due on June 30. Sarah likes her house, but her neighborhood has many problems. Sarah thinks that the government helps other neighborhoods, but not hers. She does not want to lose her house.

1. What should she do? Choose the better solution.

   a. Don't pay the tax until the government agrees to help her neighborhood.

   b. Pay the tax and write a letter of protest to the mayor and City Council members.

2. Give reasons for your choice. _____

   _____

   _____

   _____

3. Write one more solution. _____

   _____

   _____

   _____

*To check your answers, look on page 145. Record your score here.*

*Turn to page 158 and record your scores for* 🔔, 🔔🔔, *and* 🔔🔔🔔.

# Rate Yourself

**Rate yourself. Use Y *(Yes)*, S *(Some)*, or N *(No)*.**

_____ 1. I understand this unit in general.

_____ 2. I understand why government is important.

_____ 3. I know how history influenced the forming of the United States.

_____ 4. I know the purposes of government in the United States.

_____ 5. I can use what I have learned.

# 2 Check Your Progress on *Like Taking Candy From a Baby*

## ☙ Check Your Memory

**Answer the questions.**

1. What is the basis for the rule of law in the United States?

2. Name one purpose of the U.S. Constitution.

3. What is one purpose of laws?

4. What is one way the rule of law limits the power of people in authority?

5. Who must obey the laws and rules of the country?

6. Why does the United States have two houses of Congress?

*To check your answers, look on pages 146 and 147. Record your score here.*

*If your score is 4 or more points, go to ☙ ☙.*

## ☙ ☙ Make It Real

**Read the situations and answer the questions.**

1. Which of these actions would require a change in the U.S. Constitution? Why?

   a. increase the number of U.S. senators from each state

   b. change the number of people allowed to immigrate to the United States

2. A police officer arrests a man who assaulted an older woman. The police officer punches and kicks the man to teach him a lesson. Who broke the law? Explain why.

*To check your answers, look on page 147. Record your score here.*

*If your score is 4 or more points, go to ☙ ☙ ☙.*

## You Be the Judge

**Read the story. Then answer the questions.**

Ralph lives next door to Mary. He has many visitors every day. Mary thinks Ralph sells illegal drugs in his house, and she wants to protect the children in the neighborhood. However, she has not seen him with drugs.

1.  What should Mary do? Choose the better solution.

    a.  She should work with other neighbors to force Ralph to move out of the neighborhood.

    b.  If she confirms her suspicion that Ralph sells drugs, she should report him to the police.

2.  Give reasons for your choice. _____

    _____

    _____

    _____

3.  Write one more solution. _____

    _____

    _____

    _____

*To check your answers, look on page 147. Record your score here.*

*Turn to page 158 and record your scores for 🔔, 🔔🔔, and 🔔🔔🔔.*

## Rate Yourself

**Rate yourself. Use Y *(Yes)*, S *(Some)*, or N *(No)*.**

_____ 1. I understand this unit in general.

_____ 2. I understand the concept of the rule of law.

_____ 3. I understand the events leading up to the writing of the U.S. Constitution.

_____ 4. I understand the compromises that were necessary in developing the Constitution.

_____ 5. I can use what I have learned.

# 3 Check Your Progress on *For the Greater Good*

### Check Your Memory

**Answer the questions.**

1. Why did supporters of the Constitution want a strong national government?

2. What were opponents of the Constitution afraid of?

3. Why did supporters of the Constitution agree to add a bill of rights?

4. What was the purpose of the Bill of Rights?

5. Name one right in the Bill of Rights.

6. What process was followed to approve the U.S. Bill of Rights?

*To check your answers, look on page 148. Record your score here.*

*If your score is 4 or more points, go to* 🔔🔔.

### Make It Real

**Read the quote, read the situation, and then answer the questions.**

> Sometimes different groups want different things, and their rights conflict.

There is a large forest in Green County. Some people have been working for a logging company for many years. They chop down trees and sell the wood. They do not want to lose their jobs. They say that the logging brings money to the whole county. Other people want the forest to be a state park. They want a place to hike and enjoy nature. They say the logging will destroy the land and hurt the environment.

1. How could a park
   a. help individuals?
   b. help the whole community?
   c. hurt individuals?

2. How can logging
   a. benefit individuals?
   b. benefit the community?
   c. hurt the community?

*To check your answers, look on page 149. Record your score here.*

*If your score is 4 or more points, go to* 🔔🔔🔔.

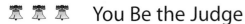 You Be the Judge

**Read the situation. Then answer the questions.**

> When different groups have different interests, someone or some group with authority must decide what to do.

Mary Jones is the principal of Jefferson School. Expenses are increasing and the school does not have enough money for next year. Many parents think that the school should end the music program because only thirty students take music classes. The music students' parents think that the program is important. They think the school should take a little money away from all the programs. Mary Jones wants to make the best decision for the whole school.

1. What should she do first? Choose the better solution.

   a. Meet with both groups of parents to hear their opinions before deciding.

   b. End the music program because program participation is so small.

2. Give reasons for your choice. _____

   _____

   _____

3. Write one more solution. _____

   _____

   _____

***To check your answers, look on page 149. Record your score here.*** ☐

***Turn to page 158 and record your scores for*** ***.***

## Rate Yourself

**Rate yourself. Use Y *(Yes)*, S *(Some)*, or N *(No)*.**

_____ 1. I understand this unit in general.

_____ 2. I understand how the Federalists and Anti-Federalists reacted to the proposed Constitution.

_____ 3. I know the purpose of the Bill of Rights and some of the rights it protects.

_____ 4. I understand some of the options people have when their individual rights conflict with the common good.

_____ 5. I can use what I have learned.

# 4 Check Your Progress on
## *Between a Rock and a Hard Place*

🔔 **Check Your Memory**

**Answer the questions.**

1. What is federalism?

2. What are the three branches of government in the United States?

3. Why is the separation of government power into three branches important?

4. Give an example of how one branch of government can limit the power of another branch.

5. What is one difference between the powers of federal and state governments?

6. How can Congress limit the president's war powers?

*To check your answers, look on page 150. Record your score here.* ▢

*If your score is 4 or more points, go to 🔔 🔔.*

🔔 🔔 **Make It Real**

**Read the situations and answer the questions.**

1. A state legislature has passed a law that makes it illegal to use a language other than English on the job. Many citizens support the new law, but an equal number are opposed to it.

   a. What two options does the governor have?

   b. What can someone who opposes the law do?

   c. What can the courts do?

2. Both houses of Congress have passed a bill that legalizes prayer in the public schools. There is strong support for the bill from a large coalition of religious groups.

   a. How can the president stop the bill from becoming law?

   b. If the president doesn't sign the bill, what can Congress do to make the bill law?

   c. How can the Supreme Court overturn the law?

*To check your answers, look on page 151. Record your score here.* ▢

*If your score is 4 or more points, go to 🔔 🔔 🔔.*

🔔 🔔 🔔  You Be the Judge

**Read the situation. Then answer the questions.**

The Heights, a very successful restaurant, is in an old house in an old section of town. It has been quite popular for many years, especially among political leaders. The entrance is at the top of a set of stairs. Since the passage of the Americans with Disabilities Act (ADA), some people have filed complaints against the restaurant with the city.

1.  What should the city do?  Choose the better solution.

    a.  Suggest ways to solve the problem, but let the restaurant continue to operate, even if it doesn't make the changes.

    b.  Issue a warning and close the restaurant if it doesn't correct the situation.

2.  Give reasons for your choice. _____

    _____

    _____

    _____

3.  Write one more solution. _____

    _____

    _____

    _____

*To check your answers, look on page 151.  Record your score here.* ☐

*Turn to page 158 and record your scores for* 🔔*,* 🔔 🔔*, and* 🔔 🔔 🔔*.*

## Rate Yourself

**Rate yourself.  Use Y *(Yes)*, S *(Some)*, or N *(No)*.**

_____ 1.  I understand this unit in general.

_____ 2.  I understand the principles of federalism and separation of powers.

_____ 3.  I know the branches of government and can identify the functions of each branch.

_____ 4.  I understand the system of checks and balances among the three branches of government.

_____ 5.  I can use what I have learned.

# 5 Check Your Progress on
## Collision Course, Part 1

### 🔔 Check Your Memory

**Answer the questions.**

1. In this episode, Sanford says, "We were once a nation united in our beliefs and values. But no longer." Is his statement accurate? Tell why or why not.

2. Name the first group of people who lived in the land that is now the United States.

3. Name one group of immigrants and explain why they immigrated.

4. Give one example of how groups of people living in the United States are different from one another.

5. What holds together the different groups of people in the United States?

6. Name one personal freedom in the First Amendment to the Constitution.

***To check your answers, look on pages 152 and 153. Record your score here.*** ☐

***If your score is 4 or more points, go to 🔔🔔.***

### 🔔🔔 Make It Real

**Read the story and answer the questions.**

The Citizens Action Group believes that their local library has offensive books on the shelves. They think the library should remove these books. The librarian does not agree. He says people have a right to read the books. The Citizens Action Group decides to protest. They talk to people in front of the library. In the library, they try to burn the offensive books. They appear on TV and say that the librarian should be fired. In an interview, the librarian calls them dangerous and frightening. They phone the librarian and tell him that if he doesn't quit his job, they will hurt him.

1. List what the Citizens Action Group did. On the left side of the chart, list their actions that are protected by the First Amendment. On the right side of the chart, list their actions that are not protected by the First Amendment.

| Protected by the First Amendment | Not Protected by the First Amendment |
|---|---|
| • | • |
| • | • |

2. Explain why the actions you have listed on the left side of the chart are protected by the First Amendment. Explain why those on the right side are not.

***To check your answers, look on page 153. Record your score here.***

***If your score is 4 or more points, go to 🔔🔔🔔.***

🔔🔔🔔   You Be the Judge

**Read the situation. Then answer the questions.**

Jane is a nurse at a clinic for pregnant women. Most of the women are immigrants. The clinic gives patients information about good nutrition. It gives them suggestions for menus with foods such as these: milk and cereal for breakfast; a tuna sandwich for lunch; and chicken with a green salad for dinner. Jane wants her patients to eat healthy food, but many patients do not use the menus.

1. What should Jane do? Choose the better solution.

    a. Tell patients that it is important to use the American menus to have healthy babies.

    b. Also offer menus of healthy foods from other cultures.

2. Give reasons for your choice. _____

_____

_____

3. Write one more solution. _____

_____

_____

***To check your answers, look on page 153. Record your score here.***

***Turn to page 158 and record your scores for 🔔, 🔔🔔, and 🔔🔔🔔.***

## Rate Yourself

**Rate yourself. Use Y *(Yes)*, S *(Some)*, or N *(No)*.**

_____ 1. I understand this unit in general.

_____ 2. I understand how the Constitution protects freedom of expression.

_____ 3. I know what First Amendment rights are.

_____ 4. I understand that freedom of expression was one of the reasons immigrants came to America.

_____ 5. I can use what I have learned.

# 6 Check Your Progress on *Collision Course, Part 2*

🔔 Check Your Memory

**Answer the questions.**

1. Which amendment protects people's rights to express their ideas and beliefs?

2. When can the government limit free speech?

3. Give an example of a "clear and present danger."

4. Why is it important to protect ideas you dislike as well as ideas you agree with?

5. What is one benefit of freedom of speech?

6. What is one example from U.S. history of an idea that people tried to stop?

*To check your answers, look on pages 154 and 155. Record your score here.*

*If your score is 4 or more points, go to* 🔔🔔.

🔔🔔 Make It Real

**The First Amendment protects "freedom of expression"—different ways to express ideas and beliefs. Read each news story summary. Then write one argument in support of the action in the news story and one argument against it.**

| News Story Summary | Freedom of Speech | |
| --- | --- | --- |
| | *In Support of Action* | *Against Action* |
| 1. Tobacco companies are forbidden to advertise on billboards. | | |
| 2. Sheriff fires deputies who did not put up signs in their yards supporting his election. | | |
| 3. City prohibits artist from exhibiting a painting that shows a riot between two ethnic groups that occurred 20 years ago. It offends some members of the community. | | |

*To check your answers, look on page 155. Record your score here.*

*If your score is 4 or more points, go to* 🔔🔔🔔.

You Be the Judge

**Read the situation. Then answer the questions.**

Sue and Harold Swenson have two teenagers who watch a lot of television. Sue and Harold are worried about the programs on TV. They think there is too much violence and sexually explicit material.

1. Using the First Amendment as a guideline, what should they do about the programming? Choose the better solution.

   a. They should try to get a law passed requiring that televisions have a device that blocks programs containing violent or sexually explicit material.

   b. They should try to get TV networks to use a rating system that tells if television programs contain violence or are sexually explicit.

2. Give reasons for your choice. _____

   _____

   _____

   _____

3. Write one more solution. _____

   _____

   _____

   _____

*To check your answers, look on page 155. Record your score here.* ☐

*Turn to page 158 and record your scores for* 🔔, 🔔🔔, *and* 🔔🔔🔔.

## Rate Yourself

**Rate yourself. Use Y *(Yes)*, S *(Some)*, or N *(No)*.**

_____ 1. I understand this unit in general.

_____ 2. I understand why it is important to protect people's rights to express their ideas and beliefs.

_____ 3. I can name examples in U.S. history when First Amendment rights were or were not upheld.

_____ 4. I know the conditions under which government can limit free speech.

_____ 5. I can use what I have learned.

# 7 Check Your Progress on *A Delicate Balance*

## ☙ Check Your Memory

**Answer the questions.**

1. Give one reason freedom of the press is important in a democracy.

2. Why do some governments want to control the press?

3. How did the founders of the United States guarantee freedom of the press?

4. Name one limit to freedom of the press.

5. Why was the trial of John Peter Zenger important?

6. Give one example of a conflict between the government and the people's right to know.

***To check your answers, look on pages 156 and 157. Record your score here.***

***If your score is 4 or more points, go to ☙ ☙.***

## ☙ ☙ Make It Real

**Read the situation and answer the questions.**

A reporter hears that the U.S. government has a secret weapon to protect the country from attack. He begins to investigate.

1. In the Virginia colony in 1682, what would a reporter have to do to publish a story like this one?

2. What would limit the reporter's ability to print a story about a weapon in colonial Virginia?

3. Today what rights does the reporter have under the First Amendment?

4. What might limit the reporter's ability to print a story about a secret weapon today?

***To check your answers, look on page 157. Record your score here.***

***If your score is 4 or more points, go to ☙ ☙ ☙.***

## 🔔 🔔 🔔 You Be the Judge

**Read the situation. Then answer the questions.**

A caller tells a reporter that a councilman accepted a bribe from a local developer. The caller will not tell his name. He is afraid to meet with the reporter. Taking bribes is illegal. The election is next week. The voters have a right to the information. Choose the better solution.

1. What should the reporter do?

   a. Ask the caller some more questions. Write a story this week about the caller's accusations so the voters can decide the truth for themselves.

   b. Make sure the information is correct before publishing the story even if it is after the election.

2. Give reasons for your choice. _____

   _____

   _____

   _____

3. Write one more solution. _____

   _____

   _____

   _____

*To check your answers, look on page 157. Record your score here.* ⬜

*Turn to page 158 and record your scores for* 🔔*,* 🔔 🔔*, and* 🔔 🔔 🔔*.*

## Rate Yourself

**Rate yourself. Use Y *(Yes)*, S *(Some)*, or N *(No)*.**

_____ 1. I understand this unit in general.

_____ 2. I understand the benefits of freedom of the press.

_____ 3. I understand the limits of freedom of the press.

_____ 4. I know why freedom of the press is essential in a democracy.

_____ 5. I can use what I have learned.

# 1 Answers for Check Your Progress on *Domino Effect*

🔔 Check Your Memory (p. 130)

Each correct answer is worth 1 point. Check your answers. For any incorrect answer, review the information. If your score is 4 or more points, go to 🔔🔔.

| | Answer | Review |
|---|---|---|
| 1. | • an organized way to protect individual rights and respond to situations that call for people to work together<br><br>• the people and institutions in society with the authority to make, carry out, and enforce laws | *Turning Points* video<br><br><br>Find Out More: Reading, What is government?, p. 8 |
| 2. | • It rescues people in times of natural disasters.<br><br>• It provides troops to defend the country against aggressors.<br><br>• It provides roads so people can travel from one place to another.<br><br>• It provides health and safety standards.<br><br>• It provides police and fire protection.<br><br>• It supports education for children. | *Turning Points* video<br><br>Find Out More: Reading, Why is government important?, p. 8 |
| 3. | • to protect the rights of individuals<br><br>• to promote the common good | *Turning Points* video<br><br>Find Out More: Reading, Why is government important?, p. 8 |
| 4. | • Parliament's passing laws without colonists having any say in the matter. | *Turning Points* video |
| 5. | • It enables people to accomplish things that cannot be accomplished alone. | *Turning Points* video<br><br>Find Out More: Reading, Why is government important?, p. 8 |
| 6. | • Power is the capacity to direct or control something. Authority is the right to use power. | Find Out More: Reading, What is the difference between limited and unlimited government? Between authority and power?, p. 9 |

Make It Real (p. 130)

Answers may vary. Here are some possible answers.

1. Each item is worth 1 point.

   a. Rescue people trapped by the water. Provide shelter for people whose homes are damaged. Help repair damage to the town. Warn people not to drink the contaminated water.

   b. Build a paved road to Millett County.

   c. Provide additional security at the airports. Try to find the people with the bomb.

2. This item is worth 3 points, 1 for the correct answer and 2 for the reason.

   No, it is not a situation of taxation without representation. The people elected the mayor and the City Council to represent their interests. The people did not like the mayor's decision, so they voted for a different mayor to represent them in the next election. The American colonists were not able to choose the government officials who made decisions about taxes.


You Be the Judge (p. 131)

Answers for questions 2 and 3 may vary. Here are some possible answers.

This question is worth 6 points, as follows:

   1 point for the better solution
   3 points for the reasons for your choices
   2 points for writing one more solution

1. **b.**

2. If Sarah doesn't pay her taxes, the government could take away her house.

3. Work with her neighbors to improve the neighborhood.

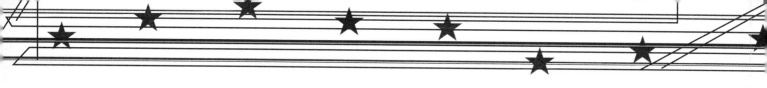

# 2 Answers for Check Your Progress on *Like Taking Candy From a Baby*

🔔 **Check Your Memory (p. 132)**

Each correct answer is worth 1 point. Check your answers. For any incorrect answer, review the information. If your score is 4 or more points, go to 🔔🔔.

| | Answer | Review |
|---|---|---|
| 1. | ● the Constitution | *Turning Points* video<br><br>Find Out More: Reading, What does "the rule of law" mean?, p. 22 |
| 2. | ● to describe the purposes of government<br><br>● to describe how government is organized<br><br>● to establish and limit the power of government<br><br>● to protect the rights of the people and promote the common good<br><br>● to provide the framework in which the rule of law operates | *Turning Points* video<br><br>Find Out More: Reading, What is the purpose of a constitution?, p. 22 |
| 3. | ● to describe how people should behave<br><br>● to protect rights<br><br>● to provide benefits<br><br>● to assign responsibility<br><br>● to limit the power of people in authority<br><br>● to protect victims of crime and people who commit crimes | Find Out More: Reading, What does "the rule of law" mean?, p. 22<br><br>Video: Mr. Tang's story |
| 4. | ● the district attorney cannot prosecute without sufficient evidence | Video: Mr. Tang's story |
| 5. | ● everyone | Find Out More: Reading, What does "the rule of law" mean?, p. 22 |

*(continued)*

| | Answer | Review |
|---|---|---|
| 6. | ● because small states wanted equal representation (each state with the same number of representatives) and large states wanted representation based on population<br><br>OR<br><br>● The decision was a compromise between small states and large states. | *Turning Points* video<br><br>Find Out More: Reading, How is government in the United States organized?, p. 23 |

## 🔔🔔 Make It Real (p. 132)

Each correct answer is worth 3 points. One point for the correct answer and 2 points for the reason.

1. **a.** The U.S. Constitution describes the form of government the country must have. It says that Congress will have two houses—the House of Representatives and the Senate. The Constitution is the basis for the rule of law.

2. Both the police officer and the man broke the law. They both committed assault. The law applies to everyone including people in positions of authority. Criminals have the right to a trial. The court decides how to punish a criminal.

## 🔔🔔🔔 You Be the Judge (p. 133)

This question is worth 6 points, as follows:

    1 point for the better solution
    3 points for the reasons the solution is better
    2 point for writing one more solution

1. **b.**

2. **b.** follows the law. The police have the responsibility of investigating crimes.

3. Answers may vary. Here are some possible answers.

   Mary could continue to watch Ralph's house. When she is sure that his activities and visitors are suspicious, she could go to the police and tell them her suspicions without involving her neighbors.

# 3 Answers for Check Your Progress on *For the Greater Good*

🔔 **Check Your Memory (p. 134)**

Each correct answer is worth 1 point. Check your answers. For any incorrect answer, review the information. If your score is 4 or more points, go to 🔔🔔.

| | Answer | Review |
|---|---|---|
| 1. | It is the only way to:<br><br>● protect the states<br><br>● guarantee the rights of citizens | *Turning Points* video |
| 2. | ● A strong national government reduces individual rights | *Turning Points* video |
| 3. | ● to get states to approve the Constitution | *Turning Points* video |
| 4. | ● to protect individual rights | *Turning Points* video |
| 5. | ● freedom of religion and expression<br><br>● right to bear arms<br><br>● right not to quarter soldiers<br><br>● security from unreasonable searches and seizures<br><br>● right of due process of law<br><br>● right to a fair trial<br><br>● right to a trial by jury<br><br>● right to fair bail and punishments | Find Out More: Reading, Bill of Rights, p. 35 |
| 6. | ● proposed to Congress<br><br>● debated, revised, and approved by Congress<br><br>● submitted to states for approval<br><br>● approved by two-thirds of states | Find Out More: Reading, What was the response to the new Constitution?, p. 34 |

**Make It Real (p. 134)**

Each correct answer is worth 3 points, 1 point for the answer to each question.
Answers may vary. Here are some possible answers.

1.  a. People could go to the park to hike and enjoy nature.

    b. A park would protect the trees and animals. It protects the land and the environment.

    c. People who work in logging could lose their jobs if the company cannot chop down the trees.

2.  a. The logging company gives people jobs and provides a product people want.

    b. The logging business brings money into the community.

    c. Logging may destroy the forests and hurt the environment.

**You Be the Judge (p. 135)**

Answers for 2 and 3 may vary. Here are some possible answers.

This question is worth 6 points, as follows:

    1 point for the better solution
    3 points for the reason for the better solution
    2 points for writing one more solution

1.  **a.**

2.  Mary Jones should try to find a way to help the whole school without hurting one group of students. She should get ideas and information from everyone before she makes a decision that affects the whole school.

3.  Look at all the school's programs. Then decide how the school can reduce spending and still offer a good education. Finally explain the decision to parents and teachers.

# 4  Answers for Check Your Progress on *Between a Rock and a Hard Place*

🔔  Check Your Memory (p. 136)

Each correct answer is worth 1 point.  Check your answers.  For any incorrect answer, review the information. If your score is 4 or more points, go to 🔔🔔.

|  | Answer | Review |
|---|---|---|
| 1. | • division of power between state and national governments<br><br>• a system that gives the federal government the authority it needs and also helps to protect state's rights | *Turning Points* video<br><br>Find Out More:  Reading, What is federalism?, p. 46 |
| 2. | • Legislative<br><br>• Executive<br><br>• Judicial | *Turning Points* video<br><br>Find Out More:  Reading, How is power separated among the executive, legislative, and judicial branches of government?, p. 46 |
| 3. | • by dividing power, there is less chance for one branch of government to abuse power | *Turning Points* video |
| 4. | • the executive branch can veto legislation that the legislative branch passes<br><br>• the legislative branch can refuse to approve appointments made by the president<br><br>• the judicial branch can rule that a law passed by the legislature is unconstitutional | *Turning Points* video<br><br>Find Out More:  Reading, How is power separated among the legislative, executive, and judicial branches of government?, p. 46 |
| 5. | THE FEDERAL GOVERNMENT<br><br>• controls trade between states and with other nations<br><br>• declares and conducts war<br><br>• prints and issues money<br><br>STATE GOVERNMENTS<br><br>• establish public schools<br><br>• enact driving regulations for state highways<br><br>• pass laws related to marriage and divorce | Find Out More:  Reading, What is federalism?, p. 46 |

*(continued)*

| | Answer | Review |
|---|---|---|
| 6. | ● Only Congress can declare war and authorize the money to support it | ● Find Out More: Reading, How is power separated among the legislative, executive, and judicial branches of government?, p. 46 |

## Make It Real (p. 136)

Each item is worth 3 points, 1 for the answer to each question. Answers may vary. Here are some possible answers.

1. a. sign the bill or veto it

   b. file a lawsuit to challenge the constitutionality of the law

   c. declare the law constitutional or unconstitutional

2. a. veto the bill

   b. vote on it again and pass it with a two-thirds majority

   c. declare it unconstitutional because it limits the basic rights of people

## You Be the Judge (p. 137)

This question is worth 6 points, as follows:

   1  point for the better solution
   3  points for the reasons
   2  point for writing one more solution

1. **b.**

2. It is the responsibility of the city to follow up on complaints. The city should issue a warning that gives the restaurant a specific time in which to correct the problem. If the restaurant doesn't correct the problem, the city should not allow it to continue to operate.

3. Answers may vary. One possible answer is that the city should investigate the complaints by visiting the restaurant to be sure that the complaints are valid before they take action.

# 5 Answers for Check Your Progress on *Collision Course, Part 1*

🔔 Check Your Memory (p. 138)

Each correct answer is worth one point. Check your answers. For any incorrect answer, review the information. If your score is 4 or more points, go to 🔔🔔.

| | Answer | Review |
|---|---|---|
| 1. | ● It is not accurate because the United States has always been a nation of immigrants with different languages cultures, and beliefs but with a shared system of values. | *Turning Points* video |
| 2. | ● Native Americans | *Turning Points* video |
| 3. | ● Africans were brought to the United States as slaves<br><br>● When the United States expanded, Spaniards who already lived in the territory became citizens of the United States.<br><br>● Mexicans when the United States expanded to include parts of Mexico<br><br>● Chinese because they heard about the discovery of gold in California and wanted to make money for their families<br><br>● Southeast Asians because of wars in their home countries | *Turning Points* video |
| 4. | ● religious diversity<br><br>● ethnic diversity<br><br>● language diversity<br><br>● cultural diversity | *Turning Points* video<br><br>Find Out More: Reading, How has the desire for freedom of expression influenced immigration to the United States?, p. 60 |
| 5. | Shared goals and values such as these:<br>● freedom of expression<br><br>● economic opportunities<br><br>● a peaceful life | *Turning Points* video<br><br>Find Out More: Reading, How has the desire for freedom of expression influenced immigration to the United States?, p. 60 |

*(continued)*

| Answer | Review |
|---|---|
| 6. ● freedom of speech <br><br> ● freedom of the press <br><br> ● freedom to gather peacefully <br><br> ● freedom to ask government to correct wrongs | ● Find Out More: Reading, What does the Constitution say about freedom of expression?, p. 60 |

## Make It Real (pp. 138 and 139)

1. Each correct answer is worth 1 point.

| Protected by the First Amendment | Not Protected by the First Amendment |
|---|---|
| ● Talk to people in front of the library. <br><br> ● Appear on TV and say the librarian should be fired. | ● Try to burn the offensive books. <br><br> ● Tell the librarian that if he doesn't quit his job, they will hurt him. |

2. This answer is worth two points.

   The First Amendment protects people's right to express their opinions. It does not allow them to threaten to harm other people or destroy property.

## You Be the Judge (p. 139)

Answers may vary for questions 2 and 3. Here are some possible answers.

This question is worth six points, as follows:

   1 point for the better solution
   3 points for the reasons for your choices
   2 points for writing one more solution

1. **b.**

2. People from different cultures eat different types of foods. There is more than one way to build a healthy diet. If patients are required to eat and cook unfamiliar foods, they may not follow the menu. Menus with familiar foods will probably be easier to use.

3. The clinic could offer cooking and nutrition classes for patients who want to learn more about healthy diets in the United States.

# 6 Answers for Check Your Progress on *Collision Course, Part 2*

🔔 Check Your Memory (p. 140)

Each correct answer is worth 1 point. Check your answers. For any incorrect answer, review the information. If your score is 4 or more points, go to 🔔 🔔.

| | Answer | Review |
|---|---|---|
| 1. | ● the First Amendment | *Turning Points* video |
| 2. | ● when there is "clear and present danger" | *Turning Points* video |
| | | Find Out More: Reading, Should free speech ever be limited?, p. 73 |
| 3. | ● when a demonstration, rally, parade, or other public event gets out of control, and puts people in danger | *Turning Points* video |
| | ● when information—such as that in classified documents—threatens the safety of the nation, as in times of war | Find Out More: Reading, Should free speech ever be limited?, p. 73 |
| 4. | ● It is important for people to be able to hear different opinions. People don't have to accept everything they hear. If government prevents the expression of some ideas, then government—not the people—is deciding which ideas are acceptable. | Find Out More: Reading, What are the benefits of freedom of speech?, p. 72 |
| 5. | ● influencing public opinion and achieving social change | Find Out More: Reading, What are the benefits of freedom of speech?, p. 72 |
| | ● hearing other ideas that promote personal growth and human dignity | |
| | ● freely exchanging ideas leads to greater knowledge | |
| 6. | ● urging the overthrow of government by force | Find Out More: Reading, When is it difficult to maintain the commitment to free speech?, p. 73 |
| | ● resisting the draft | |
| | ● encouraging mass strikes | |

## Make It Real (p. 140)

This question is worth 6 points as follows: Two points for each story, 1 point for the argument in support of the action and 1 point for the argument against the action.

1.  In Support of Action: Smoke is a hazard to people's health, so it is a danger.

    Against Action: Government cannot restrict free speech in order to control public behavior.

2.  In Support of Action: An employer should be allowed to choose his or her employees.

    Against Action: This violates the free speech of public employees.

3.  In Support of Action: Some people in the city would rather not remind others about this riot because it makes the city look bad.

    Against Action: If people don't remember this episode in history, there is a possibility that it could happen again.

## You Be the Judge (p. 141)

This question is worth 6 points, as follows:

    1  point for the better solution
    3  points for the reasons
    2  point for writing one more solution

1.  **b.**

2.  **b.** protects a person's right to watch something on TV, whether or not others agree with what specific programs show.

    **a.** violates the right to free speech. Someone has to decide what to block. It eliminates the viewer's right to decide what to watch.

3.  Answers may vary. Here is a possible answer:

    Parents can guide their children on how much TV to watch and which programs to watch, rather than using the electronic device to make those choices.

# 7 Answers for Check Your Progress on *A Delicate Balance*

🔔 **Check Your Memory (p. 142)**

Each correct answer is worth 1 point. Check your answers. For any incorrect answer, review the information. If your score is 4 or more points, go to 🔔 🔔.

| | Answer | Review |
|---|---|---|
| 1. | ● the free exchange of ideas is essential<br><br>● people have the right to know what is happening<br><br>● citizens have a right to tell government officials what they want them to do and how to do it<br><br>● citizens have a right to know how the government is performing | Find Out More: Reading, What is the role of the press today?, p. 85 |
| 2. | ● it is a way to control the thoughts and minds of people<br><br>● so people won't criticize the government<br><br>● so people won't find out what the government is doing | Find Out More: Reading, What were the challenges to the press in colonial times?, p. 84<br><br>*Turning Points* video |
| 3. | ● they included it as part of the First Amendment to the Constitution | *Turning Points* video |
| 4. | Reporters do not have the right to:<br><br>● write articles that present a clear and immediate danger to others in society<br><br>● relate information that they know is false | *Turning Points* video<br><br>Find Out More: Reading, What is the role of the press today?, p. 85 |
| 5. | ● because the jury decided he was not guilty since what he had printed about the governor was true | Find Out More: Reading, What were the challenges to the press in colonial times?, p. 84 |
| 6. | ● when the nation is at war, the release of information could endanger the troops | Find Out More: Reading, What is the role of the press today?, p. 85 |

Make It Real (p. 142)

Answers may vary. Here are some possible answers.

1. get the permission of the governor  (1 point)

2. the governor's attitude  OR  having no printing press  (1 point)

3. the right to investigate the defense system and report true information to the public  (2 points)

4. The government's responsibility for national security—security of the troops and security of the country  (2 points)

 You Be the Judge (p. 143)

This question is worth 6 points.  Answers may vary.  Here are some possible answers.

   1  point for the better solution
   3  points for the reasons
   2  point for writing one more solution.

1. **b.**

2. The press must be certain that the information in the news is true.  The reporter does not know if the caller is telling the truth.  He does not know who the caller is.  The reporter must find some way to verify the caller's accusations.  If the reporter publishes false information, he could ruin the reputation of an honest councilman.  The reporter can be charged with publishing false information.

3. Answers may vary.  Here is a possible answer.

   Ask the councilman about these accusations privately before the election and see how he responds.

# Score Sheet for Answers for Check Your Progress

| | Check Your Memory (6 points) | Make It Real (6 points) | You Be the Judge (6 points) |
|---|---|---|---|
| Unit 1 Domino Effect | _____ | _____ | _____ |
| Unit 2 Like Taking Candy from a Baby | _____ | _____ | _____ |
| Unit 3 For the Greater Good | _____ | _____ | _____ |
| Unit 4 Between a Rock and a Hard Place | _____ | _____ | _____ |
| Unit 5 Collision Course, Part 1 | _____ | _____ | _____ |
| Unit 6 Collision Course, Part 2 | _____ | _____ | _____ |
| Unit 7 A Delicate Balance | _____ | _____ | _____ |

# Glossary

**accuse**   to say that someone has done something wrong or illegal   84

**amendment**   change in a document or addition to it   34

**anarchist**   person who does not believe in government, rules, or laws   73

**ancestor**   family member who lived in past times   61

**anonymous**   not named; person whose name is withheld   81

**Anti-Federalists**   political leaders who opposed ratification of the Constitution, which they thought gave too much power to the federal government and did not protect the rights of the people   34

**appeal**   to ask a higher court to change a lower court's decision   42

**authoritarian government**   government that demands absolute obedience to its rules and laws, whether or not they are right; power usually concentrated in one person or small group   9

**authority**   legitimate right to use power   9

**benefits**   things such as medical, dental, and life insurances provided by an employer   55

**biased**   preferring one person or group over another   69

**bigot**   person with extreme opinions about race, religion, or politics   68

**Bill of Rights**   first ten amendments to the U. S. Constitution containing basic rights with which the federal government may not interfere   34

**campaign**   organized effort to achieve a result, especially in business or politics   30

**checks and balances**   sharing and balancing of power among the different branches of government so no one branch can dominate the others   46

**citation**   order to appear in court   4

**citizen**   member of a country or state; one who owes allegiance to the government and has a right to its protection and to political rights   9

**city council**   group of elected officials responsible for making a city's laws   30

**city hall**   building where a city's government is located   5

**coalition**   alliance of groups or people to achieve a common goal   43

**collective effort**   attempt to achieve a goal shared by members of a group   9

**commander-in-chief**   leader of the nation's military   47

**common good**   what is best for the entire society   8

**communist**   person who believes in a classless social and political system in which government or the people as a whole control the production of foods and goods and owns businesses and property   73

**competitive**   determined to be more successful than other people or companies   54

**comply**   to follow a rule or law   43

**compromise**   agreement reached after everyone involved accepts less than what they wanted at first   31

**constitution**   set of customs, traditions, rules, and laws that set forth the way a government is organized and operated   22

**contempt of court**   act of disobeying or showing disrespect for a court order   81

**continuance**   postponement of a hearing or trial   69

**contract**   legal agreement between two or more people or companies that tells what each side must do for the other   19

**contract**   to make an agreement to hire someone to do work   54

**controversial**   causing disagreement because people have strong differing opinions about it   69

**delegate**   person chosen to act for or represent others, as at a political convention   23

**democracy**   form of government in which political control is exercised by the people, either directly or indirectly through their elected representatives   8

**dictator**   leader of a country who has total power and controls everything   22

**disabled**   unable to use a part of the body completely; handicapped   43

**discriminate**   to treat unfairly because of prejudice based on race, sex, religion, age, or nationality   56

**district**   section of the city divided for purposes of representation on the city council   31

**documented**   supported with evidence   19

**draft resistance**   act of refusing to serve in a country's military   73

**endanger**   to put someone in a harmful situation   85

**evacuate**   to send or take all the people away from a place   5

**executive branch**   branch of government that carries out the laws made by the legislative branch; in the United States, it includes the president and his or her advisors   23

**executive power**   powers of the executive branch of the federal government   23

**federal guidelines**   specifications regarding how a law or regulation must be carried out   42

**federalism**   form of government in which power is divided between a central government and subdivisions such as state and local governments   46

**Federalists**   political leaders who supported ratification of the Constitution and a strong central government   34

**Founders**   people who played important roles in the establishment of the United States   72

**Framers**   delegates to the Constitutional Convention held in Philadelphia in 1787   23

**fraud**   illegal activity of deceiving people to get money   18

**free exchange of ideas**   right to share thoughts and beliefs without restriction   85

**free speech**   right to verbally express beliefs without government interference   57

**freedom of expression**   freedoms of speech, press, assembly, and petition that are protected by the First Amendment   60

**government**   people and institutions in a society with the authority to make, carry out, and enforce laws, and settle disputes about the laws   8

**hearsay**   something heard, but not known to be true   80

**hostage**   person kept as a prisoner by an enemy, so that the other side will do what the enemy demands   5

**illegal**   not allowed by law   19

**immigrants**   people who leave their native lands to settle in another country   60

**impeach**   to charge a public official with a crime committed while he or she is in office   47

**individual rights**   personal, political, and economic rights of citizens   8

**innocent**   not guilty of a crime   85

**judicial branch**   branch of government that interprets and applies the laws and settles disputes through a system of courts   23

**judicial review**   power of the courts to declare laws and actions of the local, state, or national government invalid if they violate the Constitution   47

**law (the)**   system of rules that people in a country, state, or city must obey   22

**law and order**   situation in which people respect the law, and crime is controlled by the police and the court system   8

**legislative branch**   branch of government that makes the laws   23

**mayor** official elected or appointed to be the chief executive of a city or town  31

**minimum wage** lowest rate that federal and state laws allow an employer to pay an employee  55

**mortgage** agreement in which people borrow money to buy a house and then pay it back gradually  19

**motion** suggestion made formally at a meeting and then decided on by voting  43

**national security** a country's obligation to protect its citizens with a strong defense force such as an army  73

**negotiate** to discuss something in order to reach agreement  4

**nomination** act of choosing someone for a particular job or to be a candidate in an election  47

**obstruction of public property** act of preventing people from entering a public building or public land that anyone can use  42

**out-of-court settlement** agreement reached outside a court of law  81

**paramedic** person trained to provide emergency medical help  5

**perfect union** best possible organization or joining of forces; group of states with the same central government  23

**permit** official written document giving someone the right to do something  56

**persecution** cruel treatment of a person or group of people because of their beliefs  60

**posterity** descendants—children and grand-children or future generations; people who will live after those now alive  60

**power** ability to direct or control something or someone  9

**Preamble** introduction to the Constitution of the United States  23

**profit** money left after deducting business expenses  54

**Puritans** members of a Protestant religious group in the 16th and 17th centuries who wanted to make religion simpler in its services and stricter in its morals  72

**ratify** to formally approve the Constitution or an amendment to it  34

**rebellion** organized attempt to change the government using violence; opposition to someone in authority  73

**refuge** place that provides shelter from danger  61

**representative democracy** system of government in which power is held by the people and exercised indirectly through elected representatives  72

**repress** to control people or ideas by force  73

**resolution** formal decision agreed on by a group after a vote  31

**right to know** being allowed access to information according to law  85

**riot** uncontrolled violent behavior by a large group  56

**rule of law** set of established, known, and accepted rules that provide order and security  22

**ruling** official decision about a legal problem  42

**scam** dishonest plan, usually to get money  18

**scapegoats** people blamed for something done by others or by a whole group  57

**security** protection against law-breaking; the things government does to keep the people of the nation safe  8

**separation of powers** division of control among different branches of government; in the United States, division among the legislative, executive, and judicial branches  46

**slander** false statements that harm a person's reputation  81

**source** person who gives information  80

**strike**   action by a group of workers to stop work due to a disagreement with management about pay or working conditions   73

**subordinate**   to put in a position of less importance   9

**subpoena**   written legal order that directs a person to appear in court to give testimony   81

**Supreme Court**   highest court in the United States; has authority to interpret laws and settle conflicts between states   23

**suspend**   to stop or take away, usually temporarily   56

**temp agency**   business that provides services of qualified workers to other businesses as needed, for limited periods of time   55

**tolerance**   acceptance or understanding of something different   61

**totalitarian government**   political system in which one political group controls everything and does not allow opposing groups to exist   9

**traitor**   someone disloyal to his country or friends   68

**treaty**   formal written agreement between two or more countries   47

**unconstitutional**   not in accordance with or permitted by the laws that govern a country   47

**under duress**   to do something because of illegal or unfair threats   19

**underground newspaper**   secretly printed and distributed information about something that has happened recently   84

**veto**   to forbid; constitutional power of the U.S. president to refuse to sign a bill passed by Congress   47

**violate**   to act against the law   68

**welfare**   money provided by the government to people who are temporarily in financial need   54

# Photo Credits

**Unit 1: Domino Effect**
Men with boat in flood waters. *Doug Menuez/Stock, Boston/PNI*
Marines planning their assault. *Jim Sugar Photography/Corbis*
Traffic on Interstate 10. *Galen Rowell/Corbis*
Nurse serves elderly woman in wheelchair. *Tom Tracy/Photo Network/PNI*

**Unit 2: Like Taking Candy from a Baby**
Baseball player sliding into base. *SuperStock*
Smart Machine radar device. *AP/Wide World Photos*
Woman in car pulled over by police for speeding. *SuperStock*
Woman feeding child. *Jennie Woodcock; Reflections Photolibrary/Corbis*
Don't Walk signal/sign. *SuperStock*
Mother and children in church. *American Stock Photography*
Children standing in school. *SuperStock*
Woman filling out tax return. *SuperStock*
President Nixon giving televised address. *National Archives and Records Administration*
Capitol Building in Washington, D.C. *Corbis Digital Stock*
White House. *Corbis Digital Stock*
Supreme Court Building in Washington, D.C. *Corbis Digital Stock*

**Unit 3: For the Greater Good**
House under construction. *SuperStock*
Children sitting in school. *SuperStock*
"Welcome to Texas" sign. *Joseph Sohm; ChromoSohm Inc./Corbis*
Pickets/State Capitol, Springfield, IL. *American Stock Photography*
Girls in colonial America listening to an outdoor political discussion. *The Granger Collection, New York*
George Washington is sworn in as first president of the United States in New York City. *The Granger Collection, New York*
"Betsy Ross" by Jean Leon Gerome Ferris. *SuperStock*
United States Flag, 1997. *Digital Vision*

**Unit 4: Between a Rock and a Hard Place**
Soldiers on reconnaissance. *American Stock Photography*
Baby receiving shot in shoulder. *SuperStock*
Mail carrier. *Lawrence Migdale/Stock, Boston*
President Clinton signing a bill. *Reuters/Corbis-Bettmann*
Federal funding interstate highway project sign. *Mark Burnett/Stock, Boston/PNI*
Capitol Building in Washington, D.C. *Corbis Digital Stock*
White House. *Corbis Digital Stock*
Supreme Court Building in Washington, D.C. *Corbis Digital Stock*

**Unit 5: Collision Course, Part I**
Man being interviewed. *SuperStock*
Union members rally. *Agence France Presse/Corbis-Bettmann*
Ballot referendum. *Michael Grecco/Stock, Boston*
Becoming a United States citizen. *Joseph Sohm; ChromoSohm Inc./Corbis*
California Cornucopia of the World. Room for Millions of Immigrants. *Collection of the New-York Historical Society*
"Ship Breaking Through Ice at the St. Lawrence Mouth." *Courtesy of the Mariners' Museum, Newport News, Virginia*

## Unit 6:  Collision Course, Part 2

Protesters yell at New York State Troopers. *AP/Wide World Photos*
An abortion-rights demonstrator shouts at anti-abortion demonstrators. *AP/Wide World Photos*
Electrical workers anti-NAFTA rally. *Joseph Sohm; ChromoSohm Inc./Corbis*
New York Democratic mayoral candidate Ruth Messinger campaigning. *AP/Wide World Photos*
Vacuum salesman seen through peephole in door. *Lien/Nibauer Photography/Liaison*
Two U.S. Communist leaders join pickets in front of federal courthouse. *AP/Wide World Photos*
Angry protester throws a rock during a demonstration. *Christopher Morris/Black Star/PNI*

## Unit 7:  A Delicate Balance

Policemen hold back cameramen. *Karoly Matusz/Sovfoto/ Eastfoto/PNI*
Censored issue of *The Rhodesia Herald. The Image Works/Topham Picturepoint*
Contemporary newspaper printing press. *SuperStock*
Anti-censorship poster in the East Village. *David Robinson/Corbis*
Workshop of an American printer. *Corbis-Bettmann*
Burning of Peter Zenger's *Weekly Journal. Culver Pictures*
Trial of John Peter Zenger. *Culver Pictures*